AF374484

Table of Contents

4

Truth Is In The Art - Original

It is in the flow of motion,

Through all the threads of time,

Twisted, turned, even broken,

Resurrected and reversed in mind.

Used by kingdoms to control,

Hidden for centuries until now,

Forgotten and remembered, never told

By those whose tongues are loud.

Now is the time to start;

Before was prophecy and inspiration

From the good and pure in heart,

The first, the last temptation.

When the world saw only one speech,

And before the tower of Babel,

Not every man could go preach;

Very few knew all was well.

"The sons of God saw daughters of men,"
And who were the sons?
They were the threads without sin,

The Adams, the Abels, the one.

This life I tell for a reason,

The time has come to reveal

Pictures in paintings, stories in seasons,

But now all things must heal.

"My spirit shall not strive with man forever,"

The sons of God are gone,

From giants on earth or whatever,

The mix was necessary but wrong.

Look in between the lines

And try to see your part;

Poetry and writing are mine,

Truth is in the art.

1
G
e
n
e
s
i
s

Metaphors... Allegories...
Poetry

In the beginning...
And G-d said let there be light...
And G-d created the firmament heaven...
And the earth was brought forth...
And for days and years...
And every living thing that moves...
So G-d created man in His own image...

nothing. first day. second day. third day. fourth day. fifth day. sixth day.

And I beheld when he had opened the sixth seal, and, lo, there was a great earthquake; and the sun became black as sackcloth of hair, and the moon became as blood;

And the stars of heaven fell unto the earth, even as a fig tree casteth her untimely figs, when she is shaken of a mighty wind.

— Revelation 6 : 12

And the Lord God formed man of the dust of the ground, and breathed into his nostrils the breath of life; and man became a living being.

And (remember) when your Lord said to the angels: "I am going to create a man (Adam) from sounding clay of altered black smooth mud.

"So, when I have fashioned him completely

and breathed into him (Adam) the soul which I created for him, then fall (you) down prostrating yourselves unto him."

—Noble Quran 15:28-29

In the beginning was the wor

d.
In
the
beg
inni
ng
the
re
was
you
.

In the beginning there was utter darkness,
And the light
proceeded forth
from that darkness.
And the light shines
in the darkness,
And the darkness did not comprehend it.

In the beginning there was black.
You were in the world, and the world was
made through you, and the world did not
know you.
You came to your own, and

your own did not receive
you. In the beginning there
was Revelation...

Behold, he is coming with clouds, and every eye will see him, even they who pierced him. And all the tribes of the earth will mourn because of him even so, amen.

— R e v e l a t i o n 1 : 7

In the beginning was the Word, and the Word was with God, and the Word was God. He was with God in the beginning. Through him all things were made; without him nothing was made that has been made. In him was life, and that life was the light of men. The light shines in the darkness, but the darkness has not understood it.

The beginning...

In the beginning we were all with Allah wherever and whenever. That was where we were, but unless you are privileged to that knowledge, you have no memory of it. The only beginning that you have knowledge of is that which has been revealed to you: the physical/material, the obvious, the here and now. The present.

The past proves itself by the effect of its outcome, and we are here as the result of our parents, and them by their parents, and so on and so on, b Allah's permission. The past also proves itself from the evidence it leaves and by the manifestation of prophecy. Before cannot be proven, only the afte as a result of the here and now, which is added up and therefore deduces th outcome.

H
i
s
t
o
r
y
P
r
o
p
h
e
c

yRevelation+Guidance_Tru

t

h

"Before Abraham was, I am."

Let us now examine this statement. When you build a building, much precedes its construction. There is first, we presume, the thought/idea and so much more before you even attempt to build the foundation. And like the building is nothing without a solid foundation, the foundation is nothin without all that precedes it. The substance of the foundation before Jesus wa the preceding prophets; they were all sent before him, yet they were for him. Allah created the world not just for him. He (Jesus) is part of our foundation however, the building that is being built is much bigger than Jesus and all of the prophets combined, which is why they were sent. Though he is one of the main aspects (i.e., a key), we are supposed to be his reflection, his students his building. Now, if you look at all of this in this light, then you can say, "Before the building was, the foundation is." In the beginning, Allah knew exactly when He was to create all of us: Jesus, Abraham, you, me, all of us. We were of His thoughts,

and His thoughts being of Him, we were with
Him We were not Him, but we were with Him.
Allah says: *Who know that they shall meet
their Lord and that they shall return to Him.*

*Do they seek other than the religion of Allah
(the true Islamic Monotheism worshipping
none but Allah Alone), while to Him
submitted all creatures in*

the heavens and the earth, willingly or unwillingly. And to Him shall they all be returned.

In the beginning, you were with Allah; you just, by His permission, cannot remember, so the statement *"In the beginning was the word...and the word was G-d"* is false and/or a mistranslation of the scriptures, because your word that is *of* you can never be you (completely) but can be only a part of you (thought/idea).

If you have a thought, isn't that thought with you, part of you? But where does the thought originate from? Even before it is made manifest, the thought is of you; therefore, if you consider yourself to be of the body (building) of Christ, then you can say, "Before Abraham was, I am." This does not make Christ any less than who he is; in fact, it makes him greater, if you only but knew.

There are things that cannot be seen without the proper understanding, that cannot be taught or learned but is simply a gift. This gift is granted to those whom it is for before they are even born, and they won't know it until situations produced by trials cause the circumstance to open this channel. This is my beginning, it is my present; this is my future, and it will, *insha Allah,* be my end. It is what I have to give, and I only wish that you allow me to share what is dearest to me.

In the beginning, I was blind, deaf, and dumb. Starting from the time I was able to discern between right and wrong, what was true, what was false, I was "ripe for the picking," and I was perfect for the plan that America had in store for me. Being the firstborn of my father and second born of my mother because of my mother's previous relationship, I was scared. I started off as a rebel for the cause of what seemed right. Having an older brother and a younger sister, I was the middle child (the black sheep). I was as bad as so-called hell, mischievously hardheaded, but Allah had a plan for me, and He is the best of planners.

The broken family, the black family, is the main family that was affected by the Willie Lynch phenomenon.

"How to Make a Slave"

(by the Black Arcade, Arcade Liberation Library, 1970, recompiled and reedited by Kenneth T. Spann)

The following treatise, to the knowledgeable, will be the missing link that has been sought to explain how we were put into the condition that we find ourselves in today. It confirms the fact that the slave holder tried to leave nothing to chance when it came to his property, his slaves. It demonstrates how, out of necessity, the slave holder had to derive a system for perpetuating his cash crop, the slave, while at the same time insulating himself from retribution by his unique property.

A careful analysis of the following "handbook" will hopefully change the ignorant among our people who say "Why study slavery?" Those narrow minded people will be shown that the condition of people is due to a scientific and psychological blue print for the perpetuation of the mental condition that allowed slavery to flourish. The slave holder was keenly aware of the breeding principles of his livestock, and the following treatise demonstrates that he thoroughly used those principles on his human live stock as well, the African Slave, and added a debilitating psychological component as well.

It was the interest and business of slaveholders to study human nature, in particular, with view to practical results, and many of them attained astonishing proficiency in this direction. They had to deal not with earth, wood, and stone, but with men, and by every regard they had, for their own safety and prosperity, the need to know the material on which they were to work.

Conscious of the injustice and wrong they were every hour perpetuating and knowing what they themselves would do if they were the victims of such wrongs. They were constantly looking for the first signs of the dreaded retribution. They watched, therefore, with skilled and practiced eyes, and learned to read, with great accuracy, the state of mind and heart of the slave, through his stable face. Unusual sobriety, apparent abstraction, sullenness, and indifference, indeed any mood out of the common way afforded ground for suspicion and inquiry. "Let's Make a Slave" is a study of the scientific process of man breaking and slave making. It describes the rationale and results of the Anglo Saxon's ideas and methods of insuring the master/slave relationship.

—
Fred
erick
Dou
glas

From "LET'S MAKE A SLAVE"

Willie Lynch
The Origin and Development of a Social Being Called "The Negro"

Let us make a slave. What do we Need?
First of all we need a black nigger

man, a pregnant nigger woman and her baby nigger boy. Second, we will use the same basic principle that we use in breaking a horse, combined with some more sustaining factors. We reduce them from their natural state in nature; whereas nature provides them with the natural capacity to take care of their needs and the needs of their offspring, we break that natural string of independence from them and thereby create a dependency state so that we may be able to get from them useful production for our business and pleasure.

CARDINAL PRINCIPLE FOR MAKING A NEGRO

For fear that our future generations may not understand the principle of breaking both horses and men, we lay down the art. For, if we are to sustain our basic economy we must break both of the beasts together, the nigger and the horse. We understand that short range planning in economics results in periodic economic chaos, so that, to avoid turmoil in the economy, it requires us to have breadth and depth in long range comprehensive planning, articulating both skill and sharp perception. We lay down the following principles for long range comprehensive economic planning: Both horse and niggers are no good to the economy in the wild or natural state.

Both must be broken and tied together for orderly production.

For orderly futures, special and particular attention must be paid to the female and the youngest offspring.

Both must be crossbred to produce a variety and division of labor.

Both must taught to respond to a peculiar new language.

Psychological and physical instruction of containment must be created for both.

We hold the above six cardinals as truths to be self-evident, based upon following discourse concerning the economics of breaking and tying the horse and nigger together...all inclusive of the six principles laid down above. NOTE: Neither principles alone will suffice for good economics. All principles must be employed for the orderly good of the nation. Accordingly, both a wild horse and a wild or natural nigger is dangerous even if captured, for they will have the tendency to seek their customary freedom, and, in doing so, might kill you in your sleep. You cannot rest. They sleep while you are awake and are awake while you are asleep. They are dangerous near the family house and it requires too much labor to watch them away from the house. Above all you cannot get them to work in this natural state. Hence, both the horse and the nigger must be broken, that is break them from one form of mental life to another, keep the body and take the mind. In other words, break the will to resist.

Now the breaking process is the same for the horse and the nigger, only slightly varying in degrees. But as we said before, you must keep your eye focused on the female and the offspring of the horse and the nigger. A brief discourse in offspring development will shed light on the key to sound economic principle. Pay little attention to the generation of original breaking but concentrate on future generations. Therefore, if you break the female, she will break the offspring in its early years of development and, when the offspring is old enough to work, she will deliver it up to you. For her normal female protective tendencies will have been lost in the original breaking process. For example, take the case of the wild stud horse, a female horse and an already infant horse and compare the breaking process with two captured nigger males in their natural state, a pregnant nigger woman with her infant offspring. Take the stud horse, break him for limited containment. Completely break the female horse until she becomes very gentle whereas you or anybody can ride her in comfort. Breed the mare until you have the desired offspring. Then you can turn the stud to freedom until you need him again. Train the female horse whereby she will eat out of your hand, and she will train the infant horse to eat of your hand also.

When it comes to breaking the uncivilized nigger, use the same process, but vary the degree and step up the pressure so as to do a complete reversal of the mind. Take the meanest and most restless nigger, strip him of his clothes in front of the remaining niggers, the female, and the nigger infant, tar and feather him, tie each leg to a different horse faced in opposite directions, set him afire and beat both horses to pull him apart in front of the remaining niggers. The next step is to take a bullwhip and beat the remaining nigger male to the point of death in front of the female and the infant. Don't kill him. But put the fear of G-d in him, for he can be useful for future breeding. THE BREAKING PROCESS OF THE AFRICAN WOMAN Take the female and run a series of tests on her to see if she will submit to your desires willingly. Test her in every way, because she is the most important factor for good economics. If she shows any signs of resistance in submitting completely to your will, do not hesitate to use the bullwhip on her to extract that last bit of bitch out of her. Take care not to kill her, for in doing so, you spoil good economics. When in complete submission, she will train her offspring in the early years to submit to labor when they become of age. Understanding is the best thing.

Therefore, we shall go deeper into this area of the subject matter concerning what we have produced here in this breaking of the female nigger. We have reversed the relationship. In her natural, uncivilized state she would have a strong dependency on the uncivilized nigger male, and she would have a limited protective dependency toward her independent male offspring and would raise female offspring to be dependent like her. Nature had provided for this type of balance. We reversed nature by burning and pulling one civilized nigger apart and bullwhipping the other to the point of death—all in her presence. By her being left alone, unprotected, with male image destroyed, the ordeal caused her to move from her psychological dependent state to a frozen independent state. In this frozen psychological state of independence she will raise her male and female offspring in reversed roles. For fear of the young male's life she will psychologically train him to be mentally weak and dependent but physically strong. Because she has become psychologically independent, she will train her female offspring to be psychological independent as well. What have you got? You've got the nigger woman out front and the nigger man behind and scared. This is the perfect situation for sound sleep and economics. Before the breaking process, we had to be alert and on guard at all times. Now we can sleep soundly, for out of frozen fear, his woman stands guard for us. He cannot get past her early infant slave molding process. He is a good tool, now ready to be tied to the horse at a tender age. By the time a nigger boy reaches the age of sixteen, he is soundly broken in and ready for a long life of sound and efficient work and the reproduction of a unit of good labor force.

Continually, through the breaking of uncivilized savage niggers, by throwing the nigger female savage into a frozen psychological state of independency, by killing the protective male image, and by creating a submissive dependent mind of the nigger male slave, we have created an orbiting cycle that turns on its own axis forever, unless a phenomenon occurs and reshifts the positions of the male and female savages. We show what we mean by example. We breed two nigger males with two nigger females. Then we take the nigger males away from them and keep them moving and working. Say the nigger female bear a nigger female and the other bears a nigger male. Both nigger females, being without influence of the nigger male image, frozen with an independent psychology, will raise him to be mentally dependent and weak, but physically strong...in other words, body over mind. We will mate and breed them and continue the cycle. That is good, sound, and long range comprehensive planning.

WARNING: POSSIBLE INTERLOPING NEGATIVES
Earlier, we talked about the non-economic good of the horse and the nigger in their wild or natural state; we talked about the principle of breaking and tying them together for orderly production, furthermore, we talked about paying particular attention to the female savage and her offspring for orderly future planning; then more recently we stated that, by reversing the positions of the male and female savages we had created an orbiting cycle that turns on its own axis forever, unless phenomenon occurred, and reshifted the positions of the male and female savages.

Our experts warned us about the possibility

of this phenomenon occurring, for they say that the mind has a strong drive to correct and recorrect itself over a period of time if it can touch some substantial original historical base; and they advised us that the best way to deal with phenomenon is to shave off the brute's mental history and create a multiplicity of phenomenon or illusions so that each illusion will twirl in its own orbit, something akin to floating balls in a vacuum. This creation of a multiplicity of phenomenon or illusions entails the principles of crossbreeding the nigger and the horse as we stated above, the purpose of which is to create a diversified division of labor. The result of which is severance of the points of original beginnings for each spherical illusion. Since we felt that the subject matter may get more complicated as we proceed in laying down our economic plan concerning the purpose, reason, and effect of cross-breeding horses and niggers, we shall lay down the following definitional terms for future generations.

Orbiting cycle means a
thing turning in a given
pattern. Axis means upon
which or around which a
body turns.
Phenomenon means something

beyond ordinary conception that
inspires awe and wonder.

Multiplic

ity

means a

great

number.

Sphere

means a

globe.

Cross-breeding a horse means
taking a horse and breeding it with an
ass and you get a dumb backward ass,
long headed mule that is not
reproductive nor productive by itself.

Cross-breeding niggers means taking so many drops of good white blood and putting them into as many nigger women as possible, varying the drops by the various tone that you want, and then letting them breed with each other until cycle of colors appear as you desire.

What this means is this: Put the niggers and the horse in the breeding or, mix some asses and some good white blood and what do you get? You got a multiplicity of colors of ass backwards, unusual niggers, running, tied to backwards ass long headed mules, the one productive of itself, the other sterile. (The one constant, the other dying. We keep nigger constant for we may replace the mule for another tool), both mule and nigger tied to each other, neither knowing where the other came from and neither productive for itself, nor without each other.

CONTROLLED LANGUAGE
Cross-breeding completed, for further severance from their original

beginning, we must completely annihilate the mother tongue of both the nigger and the new mule and institute a new language that involves the new life's work of both. You know, language is a peculiar institution. It leads to the heart of people. The more a foreigner knows about the language of another country, the more he is able to move through all levels of that society. Therefore, if the foreigner is an enemy of the country, to the extent that he knows the body of the language, to that extent is the country vulnerable to attack or invasion of a foreign culture. For example, you take the slave, if you teach him all about your language, he will know all your secrets, and he is then no more a slave, for you can't fool him any longer and having a fool is one of the basic ingredients of and incidents to the making of the slavery system.

That was their plan; now let us look at part

of the Creator's plan:

And when he had opened the fifth seal, I saw under the altar the souls of them that were slain for the word of God, and for the testimony which they held:

And they cried with a loud voice, saying, How long, O Lord, holy and true, dost thou not judge and avenge our blood on them that dwell on the earth?

And white robes were given unto every one of them; and it was said unto them, that they should rest yet for a little season, until their fellow servants also and their brethren, that should be killed as they were, should be fulfilled.

To unlock secrets or to get answers to riddles, you must know where to look and how to calculate. Our answers have always been in the scriptures as well as in the signs of Allah, but we have always run away from that which is best for us. ("Study to show thyself approved") and ("Prove all things"). Study what, prove what, whom, where, why, how? The most sensible answer would be to study ourselves, nature, and science, then parallel them with true revelation and prove that which has to do with ourselves and our lives. We are supposed to take what our parents taught us and go out into the world and prove it to be true or false—*everything,* including religion. We are supposed to be studying our parents by watching and learning what they do. If you see alcohol and drugs destroying them, that is how you learn that these things must be deleted from your lifestyle. This is to be done with every aspect of our being—diet, thoughts, it doesn't matter, the lessons are to be learned and we are to evolve from the knowledge and experience of that learning. Each generation is to take from the previous one and grow more into the oneness of Allah by conforming to what He has revealed.

In the beginning, Allah created the heavens (spiritual) and the earth (material). The material was without form, and void (empty), and darkness (ignorance) was upon the face of the deep. And the spirit (essence) of Allah was hovering over the face of the waters (sources). Then Allah said, "Let there be light (knowledge)," and there was knowledge. And Allah divided (separated) the knowledge from the ignorance. Allah called the knowledge day, and the ignorance He called night. So the dusk (evening) and the dawn (morning) were the first day.

The people answered him, We have heard out of the law that Christ abideth for ever: and how sayest thou, The Son of man must be lifted up? Who is this Son of man?

Then Jesus said unto them, Yet a little while is the light with you. Walk while ye have the light, lest darkness come upon you: for he that walketh in darkness knoweth not whither he goeth.

While ye have light, believe in the light, that ye may be the children of light. These things spake Jesus, and departed, and did hide himself from them.

—
J
o
h
n
1
2
:
3
4
—

We go on to learn that one day to Allah is as a thousand years to man. Let's look at this: The sun never goes out, so it doesn't come on. The sun doesn't rise; the earth revolves around the sun, which makes it seem as if the sun rises. So in actuality, we are still living in the first day (the beginning). We were given day and night in order to calculate time for ourselves; this is part of the reason that only He knows the hour of the end.

Now, before we go any further, I must introduce you to the **Comforter,** *"that prophet, like you" (Moses).*

*I will raise them up **a Prophet** from among their brethren, **like unto thee,** and will put **my words in his mouth;** and **he shall speak unto them all that I shall command him.***

*And it shall come to pass, that whosoever will not hearken unto my words which **he shall speak in my name,** I will require it of him.*

But the prophet, which shall presume to speak a word in my name, which I have not commanded him to speak, or that shall speak in the name of other gods, even that prophet shall die.

And if thou say in thine heart, How shall we know the word which the Lᴏʀᴅ hath not spoken?

*When a prophet speaketh **in the name of the** L*ORD*, if the thing follow not, nor come to pass, that is the thing which the L*ORD* hath not spoken, but the prophet hath spoken it presumptuously: thou shalt not be afraid of him.*

—

Deut
eron
omy
18:1
8–22

He did not fail to confess, but confessed freely, "I am not the Christ."
They asked him, "Then who are you? Are you Elijah?" He said, "I am not."
"

A
r
e
y
o

u
t
h
e
P
r
o
p
h
e
t
?
"
H
e
a
n
s
w
e
r
e
d
,
"
N
o
.

„

Nevertheless I tell you the truth; It is expedient for you that I go away: for if I go not away, the **Comforter** *will not come unto you; but if I depart, I will send* **him** *unto you.*

And when **he** *is come,* **he** *will reprove the world of sin, and of righteousness, and of judgment:*

Of sin, because they believe not in me; Of righteousness, because I go to my Father, and ye see me no more; Of judgment, because the prince of this world is judged.

*I have yet many things to say unto you, but ye cannot bear them now. Howbeit when **he**, the Spirit of truth, is come, **he** will guide you into all truth: for **he shall not speak of himself**; but whatsoever **he** shall hear, that shall **he** speak: and **he** will shew you things to come.*
*He shall glorify me: for **he** shall receive of mine, and shall shew it unto you.*

*Our beloved Prophet (peace be upon him) is called **"Muhammad"** and **"Ahmad"**. What do his names mean? Does the Prophet (peace be upon him) have other names as well? Could you give me their meanings too?*

Answered by:

Sheikh `Abd al-`Azîz b. `Abd Allah b. Muhammad Al al-Sheikh, Grand Mufti of Saudi Arabia

The word "Muhammad" is derived from the Arabic root word "hamd" meaning "praise".

It is the emphatic passive participle of that root and can be translated as "the Oft-Praised One".

As for Ahmad, is the superlative form of the same root word "hamd". It means "the Highly Praised One".

Ahmad is the name Jesus (peace be upon him) mentioned when he foretold of his coming.

Allah says: "And when Jesus son of Mary said: O Children of Israel! Lo! I am the Messenger of Allah unto you, confirming that which was revealed before me in the Torah, and bringing glad tidings of a Messenger who will come after me, whose name will be 'the Highly Praised One' (Ahmad)." [Sûrah al-Saff: 6]

The Prophet (peace be upon him) also had the name al-Mutawakkil, meaning "the one who relies on Allah".

The Prophet informs us that Allah said to him: "…and you are My servant and Messenger and I have named you al-Mutawakkil." [Sahîh al-Bukhârî]

Allah's Messenger (peace be upon him) enumerated a number of his names when he said: "I have many names: I am Muhammad. I am Ahmad. I am al-Mâhî (the Obliterator) by whom Allah obliterates disbelief. I am al-Hâshir (the Gatherer) who gathers the people at my feet. I am al-`Aqib (the Successor) whom none comes after."[Sahîh al-Bukhârî and Sahîh Muslim]

The Companion Abû Mûsâ al-Ash`arî relates the following:

Allah's Messenger (peace be upon him) called himself by many names, some of which we committed to memory and some of which we did not. He said: "I am Muhammad. I am Ahmad. I am al-Muqaffî (the Sender). I am al-Hâshir. I am the Prophet of Penitence. I am the Prophet of Mercy."

[Sahîh Muslim]

And Allah knows best.

Now let's take a look at Prophet Abraham (as)

Sarah was Abraham's first wife, but in all, he had three wives:

And Sarai Abram's wife took Hagar her maid the Egyptian, after Abram had dwelt ten years in the land of Canaan, and gave her to her husband Abram to be his wife.

And he went in unto Hagar, and she conceived: and when she saw that she had conceived, her mistress was despised in her eyes.

— Genesis 16:3

Then again Abraham took a wife, and her name was Keturah.

And she bare him Zimran, and Jokshan, and Medan, and Midian, and Ishbak, and Shuah,

— 4

— Genesis 25:1—2

Most of you probably didn't know that Abraham had more than one wife or even that he had three, since there are very few people who have read the entire Bible the way it was meant to be read (from cover to cover). There are many preachers who go around teaching the so-called word of Allah and they haven't even read the entire book that they preach from. People tend to believe that Sarah, who conceived Isaac, was Abraham's only wife; however, there was also Hagar, Abraham's second wife, who conceived Ishmael. Lastly, there was Keturah, who conceived six more sons for Abraham.

Here I'd like to focus on Sarah and Hagar. At first, Sarah could not bear any children, and thus, Hagar was the choice of Allah for Abraham's first-born.

After these things the word of the LORD came unto Abram in a vision, saying, Fear not, Abram: I am thy shield, and thy exceeding great reward.
And Abram said, LORD God, what wilt thou give me, seeing I go childless, and the steward of my house is this Eliezer of Damascus?
And Abram said, Behold, to me thou hast given no seed: and, lo, one born in

my house is mine heir.
And, behold, the word of the LORD came unto
him, saying, This shall not be thine heir; but he
that shall come forth out of thine own bowels
shall be thine heir.

Even though Ishmael and Isaac were both Abraham's seed, Ishmael was his firstborn; in fact, Ishmael was around fourteen years old when Isaac was born. Ishmael received the firstborn rights; both sons were blessed, but the prophethood would be finished through Ishmael, with Prophet Muhammad (saw) being the last prophet to mankind (peace be upon them).

Much has been revealed to man, but it was mostly done by way of parables, revelations, and the blessing of the knowledge from Allah (swt) through the sciences. This was Allah's plan to His genetically coded chosen few. If He had revealed things directly, then things would be worse than they already are. Consider Satan; he was given respite (time, power, and ability) until the Day of Judgment to be our open enemy. So just imagine if he had also been granted the advanced knowledge of Allah's entire plan. There would be no chance against the satanic forces of America or the world and what "they" have of the truth.

The truth is, in the beginning, when man was first created, he had no sin because there was no law. There was no law for man, even though there was law for everything else. The very first law for man involved disobedience to Allah's command: "Do not eat of the fruit of this tree." This was where the state of separation and awareness began with man. He was separated from his divine state and became aware of what was right and wrong. At the same time man became knowledgeable of himself, he fell from the state of felicity that he'd had, and thus, he fell from Allah's direct grace. I say "man," because "Adam and Eve" constitutes man; they are man as one and cannot be separated. When they are separated, then they become open to be a product of Satan.

Their disobedience to Allah is the beginning of man's inability to accept blame for his actions. Adam blamed Eve for his part, and Eve blamed Satan for her part, but actually, they were all at fault, especially Adam. He was Eve's husband and was supposed to be her caretaker. You see, he was present when Eve ate of the forbidden fruit, and he even partook in eating of it himself, he could have stopped her but:

And when the woman saw that the tree was good for food, and that it was pleasant to the eyes, and a tree to be desired to make one wise, she took of the fruit thereof, and did eat, and gave also unto her husband with her; and he did eat.

This is the beginning of a process of unlocking secrets and exposing the spirit and identity of America. Everything in scripture up until now is the revelation against America and her cronies (allies). The Book of Revelation is an encrypted plan of the destruction of a beast, fitting the description of a dragon, serpent, whore, etc. The book reveals all that has produced America's government and it exposes her friends and her enemies. It is not I who has judged America; it is Allah by way of the Bible and other forms of scripture, the most recent being the Holy Qu'ran: "Study to show thyself approved."

"I am Alpha and Omega, the beginning and the ending, saith the Lord, which is, and which was, and which is to come, the Almighty."

—

Revelation 1 : 8

Truth Is In The Art II

It is in his words, his signs;

channeled down and through us,

in all and what we find,

the key is faith and trust, courage, beyond belief,

thyself to show approved study,

in the night as a thief,

become the answer, the prophecy.

What you seek is delusional,

the world and all that dies,

life and all of its riddles,

then turning them into lies.

Kept from the wise and prudent,

saved unto us, the babes,

stripping the righteous of their garments,

are the Israelis on their way to Hades?

Putting them on as if they're righteous,

trying to take from the Israelites.

Genesis, Exodus, not them just-us,

them: are just pretension of supreme white.

The truth is in the parable,

to you, it might be poetry,

maybe even a little metaphorical,

but can't you see the trickery?

Time to unwind the metaphors,

replace or switch the antonyms,

knock on all the doors,

synchronize truth with synonyms.

Look in between the lines,

and try to see your part,

poetry and writing are mine,

truth is in the art.

Middle Passage

From Wikipedia, the free encyclopedia

"The Middle Passage was the stage of the triangular trade in which millions of Africans[1] were shipped to the New World as part of the Atlantic slave trade. Ships departed Europe for African markets with manufactured goods, which were traded for purchased or kidnapped Africans, who were transported across the Atlantic as slaves; the slaves were then sold or traded for raw materials,[2] which would be transported back to Europe to complete the voyage. Voyages on the Middle Passage were large financial undertakings, generally organized by companies or groups of investors rather than individuals.[3]

The "Middle Passage" was considered a   ti
me of in-betweenness for those being traded from Africa to America. The close quarters and intentional division of pre-established African communities by the ship crew motivated captive Africans to forge bonds of kinship which then created forced transatlantic communities.[4]

Traders from the Americas and Caribbean received the enslaved Africans. European powers such as Portugal, England, Spain, France, the Netherlands, Denmark, Sweden, and Brandenburg, as well as traders from Brazil and North America, took part in this trade. The enslaved

Africans came mostly from eight regions: Senegambia, Upper Guinea, Windward Coast, Gold Coast, Bight of Benin, Bight of Biafra, West Central Africa and Southeastern Africa.[5]

An estimated 15% of the Africans died at sea, with mortality rates considerably higher in Africa itself in the process of capturing and transporting indigenous people to the ships.[6] The total number of African deaths directly attributable to the Middle Passage voyage is estimated at up to two million; a broader look at African deaths directly attributable to the institution of slavery from 1500 to 1900 suggests up to four million African deaths.[7]

For two hundred years, 1440–1640, Portuguese slavers had a near monopoly on the export of slaves from Africa. During the 18th century, when the slave trade transported about 6 million Africans, British slavers carried almost 2.5 million.[8]"

Journey

"Diagram of a slave ship from the Atlantic slave trade. (From an Abstract of Evidence delivered before a select committee of the House of Commons in 1790 and 1791.)

The duration of the transatlantic voyage varied widely,[2] from one to six months depending on weather conditions. The journey became more efficient over the centuries; while an average transatlantic journey of the early 16th century lasted several months, by the 19th century the crossing often required fewer than six weeks.[9]

It is believed that African kings, warlords and private kidnappers sold captives to Europeans who held several coastal forts. The captives were usually force-marched to these ports along the western coast of Africa, where they were held for sale to the European or American slave traders in the barracoons. Typical slave ships contained several hundred   slaves with   about 30 crew members.[citation needed]

The male captives were normally chained together in pairs to save space; right leg to the next man's left leg — while the women and children may have had somewhat more room. At best, captives were fed beans, corn, yams, rice, and palm oil. Slaves were fed one meal a day with water, if at all. When food was scarce, slaveholders would get priority over the slaves.[citation needed] Sometimes captives were allowed to move around during the day, but many ships kept the shackles on throughout the arduous journey.

Most contemporary historians estimate that between 9.4 and 12 million Africans arrived in the New World.[10][11] Disease and starvation due to the length of the passage were the main contributors to the death toll with amoebic dysentery and scurvy causing the majority of deaths.[citation needed] Additionally, outbreaks of smallpox, syphilis, measles, and other diseases spread rapidly in the close-quarter compartments.

The rate of death increased with the length of the voyage, since the incidence of dysentery and of scurvy increased with longer stints at sea as the quality and amount of food and water diminished. In addition to physical sickness, many slaves became too depressed to eat or function efficiently due to loss of freedom, family, security, and their own humanity."

In the 18th century's Atlantic market economy, the need for profits drove changes in ship designs and in managing human cargo, which included enslaved Africans and the mostly white crew. Improvements in air flow on board the ships helped to decrease the infamous mortality rate that these ships had become known for throughout the 16th and 17th centuries. The new designs that allowed ships to navigate faster and into rivers' mouths ensured access to many more enslaving posts along the West African coast.[12] The monetary value of enslaved Africans in any given

American auction-block during the mid-18th century ranged between $800 and $1,200, which in modern times would be equivalent to $32,000– 48,000 apiece ($100 then is now worth $4,000 due to   inflation).
Therefore   ship captains   and investors sought technologies that would protect their human cargo.[13]

Throughout the height of the Atlantic slave trade (1570– 1808), slave ships were normally smaller than traditional cargo ships, with most slave ships weighing between 150 and 250 tons. This equated to about 350 to 450 enslaved Africans on each slave ship, or 1.5 to 2.4 per ton. The English ships of the time normally fell on the larger side of this spectrum and the French on the smaller side. Ships purposely designed to be smaller and more maneuverable were meant to navigate the African coastal rivers into farther inland ports; these ships therefore increased the effects of the slave trade on Africa. Additionally, the ships' sizes increased slightly throughout the 1700s; however the number of enslaved Africans per ship remained the same. This reduction in the ratio of enslaved Africans to ship tonnage was designed to increase the amount of space per person and thus improve the survival chances of everyone on board. These ships also had temporary storage decks which were separated by an open latticework or   grate bulkhead, Ship masters   would presumably use these chambers to divide enslaved Africans and help prevent mutiny. Some ships developed by the turn of the 19th century even had ventilation ports built into the sides and between gun ports (with hatches to keep inclement weather out). These open deck designs increased airflow and thus help   improve   survival rates, diminishing   potential investment losses.[12]

Another major   factor in "cargo protection" was the increase in knowledge of diseases and medicines (along with the inclusion of a variety of medicines on the ships). First the Dutch East India Company in the 18th century, followed by some other countries and companies in the late 18th early 19th centuries, realized that the inclusion of surgeons and other medical practitioners aboard their ships was an endeavor that proved too costly for the benefits. So instead of including medical personnel they just stocked the ships with a large variety of medicines; while this was better than no medicines, and given the fact that many crew members at least had some idea of how disease was spread, without the inclusion of medical personnel the mortality rate was still very high in the 18th century.[14]"

People tend to believe that these very significant aspects of history have little or nothing to do with what is going on today. I wish to address the most critical and diabolical of these to show the effects of what has been done and give the outcome as well as the remedy to overcome and accelerate us into the promise of Allah.

The Middle Passage is just the beginning of what black slaves experienced. There are many areas to address, but we will use only those that are pertinent to the context of this book.

Slavery (from Dictionary.com unabridged Based on the Random House Dictionary, Random House, Inc. 2006):

Noun. sley-vuh-ree

1. The condition of a slave; bondage.

2. The keeping of slaves as a practice or institution.

3. A state of subjection like that of a slave: **He was kept in slavery by drugs.**

4. Severe toil; drudgery.

A Runaway Slave

I ran, and ran, and ran…

But I ran until I just couldn't run anymore.

Lungs wouldn't breathe, gasping for air.

If I stop, my life is done for.

Needing to go on, but heart couldn't bear.

The 21st century and a brotha's still running.

From stories of slavery, both big and tall.

If you saw me, you'd say this is quite stunning,

because I got to run and hide and not look back at all;

They want me and won't stop till I'm caught.

Lord, please help me; I just want to be free.

My ancestors were already taken, sold, and bought,

And many of them still hang from a tree.

Nothing's changed, still the same, even the pain.

Mother and father are mourning in their graves.

This system I'll never submit to, it's deranged;

Well, I'm off once again, permanently a runaway slave…

Truth Is In The Art III

It is in life's puzzle.

Each piece must fit perfectly;

If not, then there's trouble.

Either way, it's still your destiny.

So easy to see and hear,

The sixth sense is to kneel.

Now taste and smell what's here;

In all of it, try to feel

The art of G-d Himself,

Shaping and molding each man

Of his spirit and health.

His mind, His work, His hand,

He created, He revealed, He healed;

The Torah, the Injil, the Qu'ran,

All from a book that's sealed.

Mercy through our sin, the song,

Tip of the hat, each artist,

In His image to create,

A clue beyond the Satanists,

Through time and again to wait.

Patiently doing their part,

The prophets, martyrs, and witnesses

Dying from the very start,

By Babylon and her accomplishments.

This song is sung to you;

He has placed it in my mouth.

See it, for it is truth;

Do not fear what it's about.

Look between the lines

and try to see your part,

Poetry and writing are mine.

Truth is in the art.

3 The Law

*The **law** of the LORD is perfect, converting the soul: the testimony of the LORD is sure, making wise the simple.*

⁷For the **law** was given by Moses, but grace

a
n
d
t
r
u
t
h
c
a
m
e
b
y
J
e
s
u
s
C
h
r
i
s

t.
— John 1:17

Think not that I am come to destroy the **law**,
or the prophets: I am not come to destroy,
but to fulfill.

— Matthew 5:

And the LORD God commanded the man, saying, Of every tree of the garden thou mayest freely eat:

But of the tree of the knowledge of good and evil, thou shalt not eat of it: for in the day that thou eatest thereof thou shalt surely die.

Law (noun)

Law [law] (*laws*)

binding or enforceable rule

a rule of conduct or procedure recognized by a community as binding or enforceable by authority

I am the LORD thy God, which brought thee out of the land of Egypt, from the house of bondage.

Thou shalt have none other gods before me.
Thou shalt not make thee any graven image,
or any likeness of any thing that is in heaven
above, or that is in the earth beneath, or that
is in the waters beneath the earth:
Thou shalt not bow down thyself unto them,
nor serve them: for I the LORD thy God am a
jealous God visiting the iniquity of the fathers
upon the children unto the third and fourth
generation of them that hate me,
And shewing mercy unto thousands of them
that love me and keep my commandments.

[1]Thou shalt not take the name of the LORD
thy God in vain: for the LORD will not hold
him guiltless that taketh his name in vain.

Keep the Sabbath day to sanctify it, as the
LORD thy God hath commanded thee.
Six days thou shalt labour, and do all thy work:
But the seventh day is the Sabbath of the
LORD thy God: in it thou shalt not do any
work, thou, nor thy son, nor thy daughter, nor
thy manservant, nor thy maidservant, nor
thine ox, nor thine ass, nor any of thy cattle,
nor thy stranger that is within thy gates; that
thy manservant and thy maidservant may rest
as well as thou.

And remember that thou wast a servant in the land of Egypt, and that the LORD thy God brought thee out thence through a mighty hand and by a stretched out arm: therefore the LORD thy God commanded thee to keep the Sabbath day.

Honour thy father and thy mother, as the LORD thy God hath commanded thee; that thy days may be prolonged, and that it may go well with thee, in the land which the LORD thy God giveth thee.

Thou shalt not kill.

Neither shalt thou commit adultery.

Neither shalt thou steal.

Neither shalt thou bear false witness against thy neighbour.

Neither shalt thou desire thy neighbour's wife, neither shalt thou covet thy neighbour's house, his field, or his manservant, or his maidservant, his ox, or his ass, or any thing

that is thy neighbour's.
These words the LORD spake unto all your
assembly in the mount out of the midst of the
fire, of the cloud, and of the thick darkness,
with a great voice: and he added no more.
And he wrote them in two tables of stone, and

delivered them unto me.

— Deuteronomy 5 : 6 — 22

O that there were such an heart in them, that they would fear me, and keep all my commandments always, that it might be well with them, and with their children for ever!

—

Ye shall not go after other gods, of the gods of the people which are round about you;

(For the LORD thy God is a jealous God among you) lest the anger of the LORD thy God be kindled against thee, and destroy thee from off the face of the earth.

*Hear the word of the LORD, ye rulers of Sodom; give ear unto the **law** of our God, ye people of Gomorrah.*

To what purpose is the multitude of your sacrifices unto me? Saith the LORD: I am full of the burnt offerings of rams, and the fat of fed beasts; and I delight not in the blood of bullocks, or of lambs, or of he goats.

When ye come to appear before me, who hath required this at your hand, to tread my courts?

Bring no more vain oblations; incense is an abomination unto me; the new moons and Sabbaths, the calling of assemblies, I cannot

*away with; it is iniquity, even the solemn
meeting.
Your new moons and your appointed feasts
my soul hateth: they are a trouble unto me; I
am weary to bear them.
And when ye spread forth your hands, I will
hide mine eyes from you: yea, when ye make
many prayers, I will not hear: your hands are
full of blood. Wash you, make you clean; put
away the evil of your doings from before
mine eyes; cease to do evil;
Learn to do well; seek judgment, relieve the
oppressed, judge the fatherless, plead for the
widow.
    Come now, and let us reason together, saith
        the LORD: though your sins be as scarlet,
they shall be as white as snow; though they
                        be red like crimson,*

they shall be as wool.
If ye be willing and obedient, ye shall eat the
good of the land:
But if ye refuse and rebel, ye shall be
devoured with the sword: for the mouth of
the LORD hath spoken it.

— Isaiah 1:10 – 20

Do not think that I have come to abolish the
Law or the Prophets; I have not come to
abolish them but to fulfill them. I tell you the
truth, until heaven and earth disappear, not

the smallest letter, not the least stroke of a pen, will by any means disappear from the Law until everything is accomplished.

*Now a man came up to Jesus and asked, "Teacher, **what good thing must I do to get eternal life?"***

*"Why do you ask me about what is good?" Jesus replied. "There is only One who is good. If you want to enter life, **obey the commandments."***

"Which ones?" the man inquired.
Jesus replied, "'Do not murder, do not commit adultery, do not steal, do not give false testimony, honor your father and mother,' and 'love your neighbor as yourself.'"
"All these I have kept," the young man said.
"What do I still lack?"
*Jesus answered, "If you want to be perfect, go, sell your possessions and give to the poor, and you will have treasure in heaven. **Then come, follow me**."*

And I John saw these things, and heard them. And when I had heard and seen, I fell down to worship before the feet of the angel which shewed me these things.

Then saith he unto me, See thou do it not: for I am thy fellow servant, and of thy brethren the prophets, and of them which keep the sayings of this book: worship God.

*They do blaspheme who say: God is one of three in a **Trinity**: for there is no* *god except One God. If they desist not from their word (of blasphemy), verily a grievous penalty will befall the blasphemers among them.*

*O People of the Book! Commit no excesses in your religion: Nor say of Allah aught but the truth. Christ Jesus the son of Mary was (no more than) an apostle of Allah, and His Word, which He bestowed on Mary, and a spirit proceeding from Him: so believe in Allah and His apostles. Say not "**Trinity**": desist: it will be better for you: for Allah is one Allah. Glory be to Him: (far exalted is He) above having a son. To Him belong all things in the heavens and on* *earth. And enough is Allah as a Disposer of affairs.*

And behold! Allah will say: "O Jesus the son of Mary! Didst thou say unto men, worship me and my mother as gods in derogation of Allah?" He will say: "Glory to Thee! Never could I say what I had no right (to say). Had I said such a thing, thou wouldst indeed have known it. Thou knowest what is in my heart, Thou I know not what is in Thine. For Thou knowest in full all that is hidden.

The Star of David, the Crucifix of Christ, and the Star and Crescent of Islam: these three ways of life are all branches that have roots coming from Abraham; however, only one of them untainted or undefiled, containing the complete law and order that was and is prescribed by the Creator.

The secrets of the so-called Jews (Zionist) and what they hold to be Judaism, the lies of the so-called Christians and what they hold to be of Christ (Christianity), the Sunnah of the (non-culturalized) Muslims and what they hold to be of Muhammad from Allah (G-d)... All exist here on earth, but only one will be acceptable in heaven. Whichever of them is not from Him will perish, and that that is from Him will continue and dominate. It will naturally consume all that there is; every knee shall surely bow and every tongue shall confess. This is the law and the command of the Almighty Allah. To not understand this is to be considered blind, deaf, and dumb.

Islam is an Arabic word that the English language distorts the definition of; in its essence, the word means to completely submit your will to do Allah's will. A Muslim is one who submits his or her will to do Allah's will. Islam is not "a monotheistic religion based on the word of Allah as revealed to Muhammad during the 7th century." This is a deception, or ignorance of those who speak English. Islam was reestablished to mankind in the seventh century by Muhammad (SAW); everything in creation has always submitted its will to do the will of Allah. Man simply lost his way somewhere between Adam and Muhammad (PBUT). The Jews were Muslim as long as they followed the law (commandments); the Christians were Muslim as long as they were like Christ. The Christians and the Jews beat, stoned, and killed their prophets and discarded what they were given by Allah from themselves:

And [mention, O Muhammad], when Allah took a covenant from those who were given the Scripture, [saying], "You must make it clear to the people and not conceal it." But they threw it away behind their backs and

*exchanged it for a small price. And wretched
is that which they purchased.*

Was it supposed to be a secret that
anyone who was considered to be a Jew was
not to be in the Twin Towers on the day that
they were destroyed? Who else knew this,
and why were the Jews the only ones to be
informed? Is it a secret that the true origins
of Israelite Jews is the tribe of Judah and that
the Israeli is not a Jew or of Jewish descent?
Is it a secret that neither Abraham nor Moses
was a Jew or Christian? Is it a secret that
none of the children of Israel were Caucasian

and therefore neither Christ, Moses, nor any of the Prophets (PBUT) was Caucasian?

If we look at just this, not even beginning to look at the other secrets or lies, where do we start with the truth? The truth must be told. It must be presented in a manner that clears all doubt and suspicion. The truth lies in the beginning, and if there is no beginning, then there is no truth.

In the beginning was the law of the Creator; obedience of His word and of His commands. If His will had been done without disobedience, we wouldn't have the problems and troubles of today; however, He allowed these problems and troubles to happen for the world to see (one day) that it is useless to try to function in any other way. This is why there are global warming, sexual diseases, and disasters, as well as many other diseases (mental, physical, social, etc.), crimes of terror, wars, and murders, to name just a few of our problems. We have strayed from the laws of our nature, which are the laws of our Creator (one world, one law, one government of Allah); we are our brothers' keepers.

The secret that the so-called Jews conceal is that of Muhammad, the last and final prophet, to the world of mankind. The true Jew knew that Muhammad was to come, and they were expecting him, but they thought that he was to be of Jewish decent. The reason they hold on to this secret is that they are of their father Satan:

*I know thy works, and tribulation, and poverty, (but thou art rich) and I know the blasphemy of them which say they are **Jews**, and are **not**, but are the synagogue of Satan.*

Behold, I will make them of the synagogue of Satan, which say they are **Jews**, and are **not**, but do lie; behold, I will make them to come and worship before thy feet, and to know that I have loved thee.

Ye are of your father the devil, and the lusts of your father ye will do. He was a murderer from the beginning, and abode not in the truth, because there is no truth in him. When he speaketh a lie, he speaketh of his own: for he is a liar, and the father of it.

— John 8:44

    If their knowledge of the truth is revealed to the world, they will lose their grip on the world. They know that what is going on between the eastern world and the western world (terrorism) has nothing to do with oil and such but is really about the rule of the three major ways of life: Judaism, Christianity, and Islam; in the last days there will be only one.

You see, these so-called Jews don't want heaven on earth. The way things were in the time of Moses wouldn't be better for them. It (the notion of heaven on earth) means nothing to them because they deal in death and profit from it.

This no longer secret information is addressed to the world because the world is the witness. Every nation has heard and seen what they have done, and the nations do absolutely nothing; therefore, they take part in the sins. Yes, they have aided in the slaughter and destruction of the black nation, and now they are trying to do the same thing to the Muslim nation, knowing once again that this nation also has done nothing in the way of harming them.

This is the day of separation, and of these you must make your choice:

Christian

i
t
y
l
s
l
a
m
J
u
d
a
i
s
m

So direct your face toward the religion, inclining to truth. [Adhere to] the fitrah of Allah upon which He has created [all] people. No change should there be in the creation of Allah. That is the correct religion, but most of the people do not know.

—

"No change should there be in the creation of Allah." There should be no change in Allah's creation, because man can only change the natural into the unnatural. Instead of man and woman as husband and wife, they all choose to allow man and man or woman and woman to be together as if they too will be man and wife, leading our children and themselves into the fire.

> *If a man has sexual relations with a man as one does with a woman, both of them have done what is detestable. They are to be put to death; their blood will*

Allah Condemns Homosexuality!

Is it man that says that homosexuality is an approved act of Allah, or is Allah Himself pleased with homosexuality? Are there any homosexuals in heaven or will there be? Was Sodom and Gomorrah a myth? Can homosexuals be fruitful and multiply? Did Allah permit man to marry man or woman to marry woman, or is this a form of man's freedom for himself? It is natural for a man and woman to conceive and produce; however, if man were left to be with man, the world would die, because this act is unnatural and is of Satan. We are created beings. Even the act of sodomy with a woman is unnatural and condemned by Allah. The world is dying because of many unnatural acts committed by man and for every unnatural act is a unnatural reaction whether we see the sign of it in the scriptures or in the course of unnatural storms and weather patterns:

> *The two angels arrived at Sodom in the evening, and Lot was sitting in the gateway of the city. When he saw them, he got up to meet them and bowed down with his face to the ground. "My lords," he said, "please turn aside to your servant's house. You can wash your feet and spend the night and then go on your way early in the morning."*
>
> *"No," they answered, "we will spend the*

night in the square."

But he insisted so strongly that they did go with him and entered his house. He prepared a meal for them, baking bread without yeast, and they ate. Before they had gone to bed, all the men from every part of the city of Sodom—both young and old—surrounded the house. They called to Lot, "Where are the men who came to you tonight? Bring them out to us so that we can have sex with them."

Lot went outside to meet them and shut the door behind him and said, "No, my friends. Don't do this wicked thing. Look, I have two daughters who have never slept with a man. Let me bring them out to you, and you can do what you like with them. But don't do anything to these men, for they have come under the protection of my roof."

"Get out of our way," they replied. "This fellow came here

*as a foreigner, and now he
wants to play the judge! We'll
treat you worse than them."
They kept bringing pressure on
Lot and moved forward to break
down the door.*

*But the men inside reached out
    and pulled Lot back into the
house and shut the door. Then
they struck the men who were
                            at*

the door of the house, young and old, with blindness so that they could not find the door.

The two men said to Lot, "Do you have anyone else here— sons-in-law, sons or daughters, or anyone else in the city who belongs to you? Get them out of here, because we are going to destroy this place. The outcry to the LORD against its people is so great that he has sent us to destroy it."

So Lot went out and spoke to his sons-in-law, who were pledged to marry his daughters. He said,

"Hurry and get out of this place, because the LORD is about to destroy the city!" But his sons-in-law thought he was joking.

With the coming of dawn, the angels urged Lot, saying, "Hurry! Take your wife and your two daughters who are here, or you will be swept away when the city is punished."

When he hesitated, the men

grasped his hand and the hands of his wife and of his two daughters and led them safely out of the city, for the LORD was merciful to them. As soon as they had brought them out, one of them said, "Flee for your lives! Don't look back, and don't stop anywhere in the plain! Flee to the mountains or you will be swept away!"

But Lot said to them, "No, my lords, please! Your servant has found favor in your eyes, and you have shown great kindness to me in sparing my life. But I can't flee to the mountains; this disaster will overtake me, and I'll die. Look, here is a town near enough to run to, and it is small. Let me flee to it—it is very small, isn't it? Then my life will be spared." He said to him, "Very well, I will grant this request too; I will not overthrow the town you speak of. But flee there quickly, because I cannot do anything until you reach it." (That is why the town was called Zoar.)

By the time Lot reached Zoar, the

sun had risen over the land. Then the LORD rained down burning sulfur on Sodom and Gomorrah—from the LORD out of the heavens. Thus he overthrew those cities and the entire plain, destroying all those living in the cities—and also the vegetation in the land. But Lot's wife looked back, and she became a pillar of salt.

Early the next morning Abraham got up and returned to the place where he had stood before the LORD. He looked down toward Sodom and Gomorrah, toward all the land of the plain, and he saw dense smoke rising from the land, like smoke from a furnace.

So when God destroyed the cities of the plain, he remembered Abraham, and he brought Lot out of the catastrophe that overthrew the cities where Lot had lived.

—
Ge
nes
is
19:
1–
29

So now, what do you believe that Allah is going to do to this world? He destroyed Sodom and Gomorrah for the homosexual sickness of those two cities but now the world is filled with much worse. Look at how the world thinks, and see how man has determined what is right and what is wrong.

Who called the preachers to preach to the people? What qualifications do they have? Why does their message differ from the messages of the Prophets? Why do they pick and choose what they want to accept of Allah's word and then compromise any or all of it to satisfy their peers? They're obviously taught by those who sold out to governments and continue to do so for a dollar. This world is on a course toward total destruction, but the kicker is that many are deceived to think that they are or will be saved. Look at all that is happening everywhere, and compare it to what is written in the scriptures. Who were you taught by? Why do you believe in what you believe? Have you truly studied, or were you given fairy tales by your parents and peers and churches? We all will soon have to answer these questions and will be called to account for our beliefs and actions. Who will you allow to guide you to heaven or hell? Will you control your own destiny and "study to show thyself approved"?

T
h
e
c
a
l
m
b
e
f
o
r
e
t
h
e
s
t
o
r
m
Is

t
h
e
tr
a
n
q
u
ili
t
y
i
n
t
h
e
a
ir
,
The
passing
seasons,
mostly
warm,

Violent
times
when no
one
cares.
Unnatur
al things
taking
over,
Homosex
uals are
reproduc
ing.
Fruitful
was the
born
order,
Multiplyi
ng faster
than
adding.
You'd
think
natural

was HIV,
And
sodomy
is not
iniquity.
But if
you
master
the
ABCs,
You'd
see the
sign in
Lot's
story;
Sodom,
and
yes,
Gomor
rah,
Egypt
of
Moses'
time,

Myster
y
Babylo
n of
Americ
a, Her
judgme
nt is
not
denied.
So
much
blood,
too
much;
Where
in it do
you
stand?
What
part
have
you
touche

d? Pledgi
ng allegia
nce to her
land? Well,
the party
is now
over, Proph
ecy is being
fulfille
d. All guilty
shall not be
sober; They
will drink

131

of
death
's still.
But it
will
not
happ
en
instan
tly; It
will
stir
round
and
round
, Build
up
from
calm'
s
myste
ry,
And
start

from
holy
groun
d.

W
e
a
t
h
e
r

i
s

j
u
s
t

o
n
e

f
a
c
t
o
r
,

N
a
t
u
r
e
,
a
ll
w
it
h
n
o
r
e
s
t
,
T
h
e
w
r

a
t
h
o
f
t
h
e
C
r
e
a
t
o
r
,
His mercy: just before the
tempest.

Truth is In The Art IV

All ahead, nothing but the end,

Life, then, to die: heartbreaking?

Let's say, depending on sin,

Is it the end or just the beginning?

Heaven to start, or maybe hell;

The hour, who knows the judgment?

Of it, this was told to tell,

Art-filled, truly Allah-sent.

Job, Psalms, Song of Solomon, Lamentations,

In scripture, twins are made desolate.

Prophecy in the book of Revelation,

Poetry, truth in history: constant.

A warrior, the writer Shelley L. Davis,

The IRS recalls this rare flower,

Her art revealed in her pages,

Of a secret culture of unbridled power.

Many have tried to unbind you,

Yet still you refuse to see;

Time is gone; it is new,

Righteous is what you must be.

To guide the nations,

And then, in turn, the worlds,

Leaders must, without hesitation

Put Allah back into the details.

If not, then lose your end.

What was learned is oh, so lost;

Babylon, because of your sin,

Others will benefit from its cost.

Look between the lines

And try to see your part.

Poetry and writing are mine.

Truth is in the art.

4
United Snakes of America

To whom it may concern,

"Oh, say can you see!?" what you have done, what you are doing, or do you even care? You're aiding and abetting the worse nation ever to exist on this planet. You are helping her with genocide, murder, slavery, rape, and many other wicked acts. By not speaking out against the unjust and inhumane use of jails and institutions, entrapment by governmental distribution of drugs, disease, their unequally directed dissemination of health care, jobs, education and all else to glorify and retain their ill-gained material and wealth, you are inadvertently if not directly guilty of the same crimes.

You are guilty! The time is at hand, and your soul is accountable. Most of you know this to be true, and still you do nothing. If you don't know, then let me show you:.

Look at the Indian nation and what was done. The black nation is insane, and they are not themselves; this too you have done. Hiroshima and Nagasaki, Afghanistan, Iraq, and on and on and on. All of this and more you have done indirectly by allowing the injustices to continue.

The blood in your veins contains your ancestors' blood. The riches you have are from the torment they have caused. The world of today is your creation, and in all of its terror you sit back and do nothing except cause more terror. Your armies kill innocent people all over the world, and you say and do nothing. With your science, religion, whatever, you destroy what Allah has created.

The facts, history, and truth, though all of the portraying of it is distorted it is now being revealed to the point of exposing the main sources of it to all of the entities involved in the destruction of the original plan and original people of Allah. This is the time of the world when all is being fulfilled; change is in effect so the world will become new.

The facts of the poverty level and the intended direction of poverty toward certain races, the jails that are constructed for the same, drugs that are

142

aimed at them, and everything else that is used to undermine the Black race in particular I am a product of. I who traveled in this world and experienced it all, saw it all, felt it all. The pain, the hurt, the degradation of this race simply for greed, power, and a false sense of superiority claimed by a wicked people. I had to go out into this world and as a victim be shaped and molded with anger and hate in order to understand how to overcome the effects of what America intended.

There is a natural enmity between Blacks and Caucasians:

> *And the LORD God said unto the serpent, Because thou hast done this, thou art cursed above all cattle, and above every beast of the field; upon thy belly shalt thou go, and dust shalt thou eat all the days of thy life:*
>
> *And I will put enmity between thee and the woman, and between thy seed and her seed; it shall bruise thy head, and thou shalt bruise his heel.*

You see, the serpent is a system or a way of thinking that is naturally ingrained in some people. This way of thinking goes back to the beginning (Genesis) and was introduced into a people and continued through they're seed even to this very day. The serpent (people) and his way of thinking (evil) has put a system in place (United Snakes) that has evolved into classism but the thing is that there is even racism in it. In order to understand the way things are propagated today you have to understand the origin of the idea. The original man or first man (Adam) was Black (we can all agree to disagree) or we can simply disagree.

And (remember) when your Lord said to the angels: "I am going to create a man (Adam) from sounding clay of altered black smooth mud.

"So, when I have fashioned him completely and breathed into him (Adam) the soul which I created for him, then fall (you) down prostrating yourselves unto him."

— Noble Quran 15:28-29

At that time Jesus answered and said, I thank thee, O Father, Lord of heaven

*and earth, because thou hast hid these things
from the wise and prudent, and hast revealed
them unto babes.*

    Now, don't get me wrong because I have
brothers and sisters who I love dearly that are
Caucasian. Likewise, even before Willie Lynch
there were many of my race who were devils.
Here's the thing, if you haven't submitted
your will to do the will of Allah (SWT) (God)
then you are contrary to His will and who else
does that if not His enemy. If you do this out
of ignorance, then you're not an enemy and it

is still according to His will. However, the system of Shaytan is a totally different entity and to be of it is a matter of choice that entails arrogance, pride, hate, envy, oppression, murder, deceit, etc., etc., etc... And this is the root cause of the impact that America has burdened the Blackman with. Also, the color of your skin doesn't make you inferior or superior, whether Black, Caucasian, Brown, whatever:

> *The Prophet Muhammad (peace be upon him), during his Last Sermon in Minâ, said:*
>
> *"O people! Your Lord is one Lord, and you all share the same father. There is no preference for Arabs over non-Arabs, nor for non-Arabs over Arabs. Neither is their preference for white people over black people, nor for black people over white people. Preference is only through righteousness." Then he said: "Have I conveyed the message?" and the people declared that he had. [Musnad Ahmad (22391)]*

Now, let's take a closer look at the idea of these

United Snakes:

Abraham Lincoln, president:
"There is a physical difference between the white and the black races which I believe will forever forbid the two races living together... While they do remain together there must be the position of superior and inferior, and I as much as any man am in favor of having the superior position assigned to the white race."

Thomas Jefferson, president:

"I advance it, therefore, as a suspicion only, that the blacks, whether originally a distinct race or made distinct by time or circumstance, are inferior to the whites in the endowments of both body and mind."

Benjamin Franklin, scientist:
"Why increase the sons of Africa, by planting then in America, where we have so fair an opportunity, by excluding all blacks and tawnys, or increasing the lovely white and red?"

Henry Berry, Virginia house of representatives:
"We have, as far as possible, closed every avenue by which the light may enter the slave's mind. If we could extinguish the capacity to see the light, our work will be complete. They would then be on the level of the beast of the fields and we then should be safe."

It was there since the beginning and it has evolved to the point of causing the Black race to have enmity between even themselves:

"Let's make a slave." This is what America has become:

> **"Recent revelations published on the Press TV website, the New York Post and Veterans Today have changed history.**
>
> The story was simple, two American congressional representatives were allowed to read the Congressional 9/11 Investigation Report, this time including the areas President Bush had ordered removed. Both congressmen clearly

state that the redacted pages of the report place full responsibility for the planning and execution of 9/11 on one or more foreign intelligence agencies, not "terrorists."

What is also clear is that President Bush's

personal role in covering this up protected the real perpetrators of 9/11 and pushed the US into, not just two insane wars but draconian moves against America's government.

The NSA and the Bush 9/11 coup

Nine eleven was a coup against the constitution. Additional reports released this week make clear some of the reasons Bush lied to the American people, to congress, our military and our allies,
  "Obama's Director
  for National Intelligence, James Clapper, has declassified new documents that reveal how the NSA was first given the green light to start collecting bulk communication data in

the hunt for Al-Qaeda terrorists after 9/11.

President Barack Obama's administration has for the first time publicly confirmed 'the existence of collection activities authorized by President George W. Bush,' such as bulk amounts of Internet and phone metadata, as part of the 'Terrorist Surveillance Program' (TSP). The disclosures are part of Washington's campaign to justify the NSA's surveillance activities, following massive leaks to the media about the classified programs by former NSA contractor Edward Snowden.

Clapper explained on Saturday that President

George W. Bush first
authorized the spying in
October 2001, just weeks
after the September 11
attacks."

We can prove Bush was
fully criminally culpable
in covering the tracks of
those responsible for
9/11.

AIPAC through Bandar and bush "under a bus"

More frighteningly, the articles published this week in Rupert Murdoch's New York Daily News, written by Hoover Institute fellow and AIPAC member, Paul Sperry, now not only blame Prince Bandar of Saudi Arabia as the 9/11 mastermind but tie Bush (43) in as well.

In fact, the entire AIPAC apparatus, the largest lobbying organization in Washington, is currently engaged in a "full court press," to stop congress from pushing for the release of the real report. Is this because the real report accuses Israel, not Saudi Arabia,   and

AIPAC wants the Murdoch/Sperry story to stand?

Bin L aden myth "crashes down"

The real report, called "shocking" by the legislators, who have called for President Obama to declassify the entire report, proves that there was no al-Qaeda involvement, no reason to invade Afghanistan or Iraq and no reason to hunt CIA operative, Colonel Tim Osman, also known as "Osama bin Laden."

In fact, Ambassador Lee Wanta, a former White House Intelligence Chief and Inspector General of the Department of Defense under Reagan, has cited meetings between key government officials and "bin Laden" that he attended, meetings held in both Los Angeles and Washington DC while the US was supposedly hunting him.

From Wanta, who was present during these

meetings,

"In early 1990, bin Laden, suffering from advanced kidney disease, was flown to an American facility in the Persian Gulf. From there, bin Laden flew to Los Angeles, landing in the Ontario airport, met by Albert Hakim, representing President Bush (41), Ollie North (free on appeal bond), Admiral William Dickie, attorney Glenn Peglau and General Jack Singlaub, one of the founders of the CIA. Hakim was the personal representative of President Bush and in overall charge of the project. 'Bud' McFarlane, an Iran-

Contra figure pardoned by President Bush in 1992, was also a part of the group.

Bin Laden then left Los Angeles for Washington DC. There he stayed in the Mayflower Hotel. Meetings were held at the Metropolitan Club in Washington. Attorney Glenn Peglau stayed at the Metropolitan. While there, Peglau's room was broken into and "items" removed. At no point is there record, classified or public, that this 'working group' was ever dissolved nor is there any record that Osama bin Laden's status as a security operative working for the US government ever ended. In 2001,

Osama bin Laden's last public statement denied any involvement in the 9/11 attacks. There are no classified documents tying bin Laden to 9/11 or citing him to be a 'rogue CIA operative.'"

Which 9/11 is real?

In 2007, the FBI flew a team to Bangkok to interview former Soviet nuclear intelligence specialist Dimitri Khalezov. Khalezov told the

FBI that, in the morning of September 12, 2001, he attended a breakfast gathering with Mossad Operations Chief Mike Harari and his son along with other Israeli operatives.

Khalezov reported to the FBI that this gathering was to celebrate the 9/11 attacks, not as Netanyahu had said, as a "fortunate happenstance for Israel" but as a Mossad attack on the United States. At that meeting, Harari also claimed credit for a role in the Oklahoma City bombing. According to Khalezov, Harari was courting him to join their group for an upcoming operation, a bombing attack on Bali, scheduled for 2002.

On October 12, 2002, a huge explosive device devastated nearly a square mile killing 202 people. An Islamic group was blamed, just as with not just 9/11 but, initially, Oklahoma City as well.

Khalezov told FBI agents that Harari claimed nuclear weapons were used to bring down the twin towers on 9/11. Harari also said he got a "cruise type" missile, a Soviet "Granit" for the Pentagon attack, purchased through Victor Bout, the "Lord of War" played by Nicholas Cage in the film of the same name.

Bout, residing in Bangkok with Harari and Khalezov,

was extradited to the United States based on a highly classified indictment accusing him of supplying the guided missile used to attack the Pentagon on 9/11. Bout was arrested in Bangkok in 2008, not long after the FBI visit. He was officially convicted of supplying arms to rebels in Colombia, an activity Bout had long

been engaged in on
behalf of the CIA, his
arms dealing partners for
many years.

L eaks

Thus far, the initial report
to congress on the Bush
falsification does not
qualify as a leak. Only
  Bush stands
  accused, the 9/11
perpetrators are still safe,
their identities still
protected by security
protocols maintained by
President
  Obama, despite
  congressional
demands.

"Claimed" leaks
          reported   by Spe
rry   in
theWashington   Post
blame Bandar and Saudi

Intelligence for 9/11. Sperry cites the CIA as a source but, quite suspiciously, seems to be attempting to deflect the possible fallout against Israel when or if then real report is made public. The Sperry story, coordinated with AIPAC's moves to quell congress's demand to declassify the report may well be an indication that Israeli intelligence, as Khalezov indicates, worked with Bush to plan and execute 9/11.

From the Press TV article: "This week, Congressional representatives Stephen Lynch (D-MA) and Walter Jones (R-NC) have officially requested a con gressional resolution demanding President Obama declassify the heavily redacted Congressional Investigative Report on 9/11. The two representatives had just been given authority under penalty of 'national security secrecy' to read the censored 28 pages of the 800-page report that had not been seen. What has been made clear is that President

Bush was fully aware that neither Afghanistan nor Iraq were involved in 9/11 and that military action against those two nations was done to cover involvement of his administration in 9/11, involvement that included support from foreign intelligence agencies.

The representatives, while reviewing the report, came to the portion titled 'Specific Sources of Foreign Support.'

A 28-page section here had been 'butchered' by the White House on the personal orders of President Bush. On the original report given to Congress, an estimated

5–10,000 words were omitted from this section with page after page of dotted lines replacing text."

This is only the most recent of revelations that AIPAC has managed to suppress through pressuring congress and its powerful assets in the press. What is increasingly clear is that many of AIPAC's allies in Washington had access to the non-redacted report. An entire administration, leaders in congress and the Pentagon, the CIA, NSA and a dozen other organizations, all knew what was in the congressional report. They all lied to the 9/11 Commission. They all ordered measures to

suppress freedom at
home and to butcher
hundreds of thousands
around the world, kidnap
and torture thousand
more, all based on lies.

Countries were virtually wiped off the map on a
whim. Often we hear it asked, "How could
thousands be involved in a conspiracy so
heinous?" We now stand ready to answer. The
time has come to ask."

Enmity

I know America stood tall,

A serpent of the dragon's lair;

I know wicked nations must fall,

Killing those of inspired air.

I see why the prophetic stall,

I pray she just lay dead there.

I guess if I'd known it all,

I'd mess around and tell it.

I don't want any of the credit.

I want her to feel this shit.

Who says it wasn't their plot?

You whore, Babylonian blood clot.

You saw only what was there.

You thought your mind was clear;

You thought the sun was hot.

You thought—or was it feared?—

You thought she was terrific.

You thought...you thought...

I am a piece of the historic;

You are, and you are not.

You see, "you" don't want heaven on earth. The way things are couldn't be better for you. The crime, poverty, and disease all means absolutely nothing to you because you know where it all comes from and you still sit back and let America continue her oppressive death dealings. This information and accusation is aimed at the world, but more specifically, it is aimed at "you". It is no longer a secret what she (America) has done; there is far too much to mention and not enough ink or paper in this book. Even the world takes part in what she does, every nation has heard and seen. Unless and until you stand up, speak out, do something, then you are, along with those millions and billions looking the other way, a spineless, moral-less hypocrite. You are her partner, and you share in her sins. You have aided her in the slaughter of the Indian nation. You have lynched, raped; you have destroyed the African nation. You have bombed the Japanese nation. You introduced terror to the Iraqi nation as well as the Afghanistan nation. *You*, the citizen, are a member of a small yet significant piece to the puzzle. You help with your lack of help for those who are truly in dire need. There is no doubt about it, you are guilty. I'm not the judge; I'm not in any position to do such a thing. This is not something that someone told me, nor is it a feeling that I have as a result of the past or present. No, it's none of those things. What you will find out, though, is that according to what is contained in all of the scriptures, the Book has judged you—or, better yet, you are being judged. There's no need for a long-drawn-out trial; the only thing that is necessary now is sentencing. History has recorded the evidence; though there are a lot of discrepancies, there is much more documented—truth to whom it may concern:

Every owner of slaves, wherever possible, ensures that his slaves belong to as many ethno linguistic groups as possible. If they cannot speak to each other, they cannot then foment rebellion and revolution.

"Every slave caught speaking his native language shall be severely punished. Where necessary, removal of the tongue is recommended. The offending organ, when removed, should be hung high in a control place, so that all may see and tremble.

Are you innocent? Or are you guilty of the crimes your country has committed? If you were innocent, then the Indian race would not be almost extinct. Most of the world hates you; take a poll and see just how much of America is loved. You sit back and enjoy the many things that your forefathers stole, raped, and plundered. Yes, their blood is in your veins, and the victims' ancestors' blood is in theirs. There must be a reason that the Creator set things up the way that they are, and there must be a certain outcome that only He and those He has chosen know.

In my blood is the pain that my people endured through the horrific times of slavery. I will never forget their cries, their suffering, and I must do what I have been chosen to do because I am a conscious unwavering result of their prayers. Though I'm told to forgive and forget, the things that I would choose to forgive cannot happen because the things that were to be forgiven have been eclipsed by other things more horrific. Forgive for the past? Look at the present and see how we have been made into fools for forgiving and/or forgetting.

I have been caught in the snares of

America's racism, yet I was supposed to be smarter than that; I was, but I had no structure, no discipline, I was like a rebellious slave and thought that I could get over (i.e., beat) the system. If I could do it all over again, I would do it exactly the same, because I am who I am and I truly believe that I'm headed to paradise as long as I now stay focused on my destiny (a witness, exposing all that I can to the children).

Islam is what America fears most, and it is what Satan knows to be the end of his reign. Total submission to Allah's will is what Allah has allowed for us not to do since the beginning of time. He allowed this so that we would learn that without total submission, we would be doomed by living in a world that has no true purpose, a life of vanity, and that we would destroy ourselves in an imperfect world. We would rise, nation after nation, repeating the same as the previous nation, treating the people like sh-t, falling victim to our lower desires and blindly leading each other in false directions toward what we view as paradise. In the end, we would finally learn that the best way and the only way was the way that it was (meant) in the beginning. That is the only thing that can succeed in guiding a nation to endure forever. Every nation has a term; the United Snakes of America has finally come to the end of hers.

Doom and Damnation

Wake all the soldiers; there is a revolution,

The end of this world: doom and damnation.

Our Lord has finally fulfilled His Revelation,

And He's here only for the worthy's salvation.

The United Snakes of America and her plantations

Will be destroyed, along with all her corporations,

The Europes, Georgias, Israelis, and other stations,

Her allies abroad, whether warring or on vacation.

Muslims, all righteous Jews, and Christians,

This is not a game; put down the Play Stations.

A wrong choice determines your termination;

No more mercy or grace; no, it is killing season.

Sound the alarms to all the righteous nations

And choose to fight for this day of separation.

Don't despair; rejoice and denounce temptation.

Reap your reward by taking the head of this dragon.

Our Lord has finally fulfilled His Revelation;

It is finished; Amen: Doom and Damnation.

Every day, we (Black Americans) have to deal with the constant roadblocks, all of the wicked obstacles and satanic snares that Caucasian America has set up against us and our people. There was and is so much hatred from the Caucasian race toward the Black race that it causes them to, by any means necessary, stop, hinder, or kill us in order to keep us from progressing. In doing so, their hatred causes them to bring harm to some of their own people, as well as other people. If you saturate a place with drugs (the ghetto) in order to cripple the people of that place by making as many of them as you can to become addicts or dealers, the connection between these people and others (poor white trash) will be the link to the source of drugs that will eventually, like a virus, affect and/or contaminate all. This is a small example of what they have always done towards Black people. Now things are really bad, things are to the point that Caucasians cannot focus only on the demise of Blacks. They have messed things up so bad, and not only that, it keeps getting worse. Even if there was a chance to fix this mess, they couldn't because they are thieves and are constantly stealing from themselves. The man of perdition can't fix the problem because he doesn't trust himself. He has robbed all areas of government and business, embezzled, tricked, and conned. They have completely broken their own system; they don't know what to do, they are hoping and now expect for a Black man, as president, to fix it. Those are the ones that want it fixed. However, there is a group of them that do not want it fixed, their intention is to destroy the whole of the world.

Anyway, they are hoping that this Black man, as president, will fix the problem; if he can, then their objective will be to steal from him his ways of doing so. There are key figures in government that are there anonymously and openly to complicate things for your president. When it is all said and done, they will try to steal and keep from giving him the credit for whatever. The way that the world works and the things of this world belong to who it [the system (Satan)] does and this is the same way that they intend on keeping it. Just like our ancestors' inventions that were stolen and/or taken from them. Though he (Barack Obama) was there and played a major role, in the end he will not be acknowledged.

<u>**www.itsabouttimebpp.com**</u>

"From The File

A "Black" Man, A Moor, John Hanson

Was the First President of the United States! 1781-1782 A.D.

George Washington was really the 8th President of the United States! George Washington was not the first President of the United

States. In fact, the first President

of the United States was one John Hanson. Don't go checking the encyclopedia for this guy's name – he is one of those great men that are lost to history. If you're extremely lucky, you may actually find a brief mention of his name.

The new country was actually formed on March 1, 1781 with the adoption of The Articles of Confederation.

This document was actually proposed on June 11, 1776, but not agreed upon by Congress until November 15, 1777. Maryland refused to sign this document until Virginia and New York ceded their western lands (Maryland was afraid that these states would gain too much power in the new government from such large amounts of land).

Once the signing took place in 1781, a President was needed to run the country. John

Hanson was chosen unanimously by Congress (which included George Washington). In fact, all the other potential candidates refused to run against him, as he was a major player in the revolution and an extremely influential member of Congress.

As the first President, Hanson had quite the shoes to fill. No one had ever been President and the role was poorly defined. His actions in office would set precedent for all future Presidents.

He took office just as the Revolutionary War ended.

Almost immediately, the troops demanded to be paid. As would be expected after any long war, there were no funds to meet the salaries. As a result, the soldiers threatened to overthrow the new government and put

Washington on the throne as a monarch.

All the members of Congress ran for their lives, leaving Hanson as the only guy left running the government. He somehow managed to calm the troops down and hold the country together. If he had failed, the government would have fallen almost immediately and everyone would have been bowing to King Washington. In fact, Hanson sent 800 pounds of sterling silver by his brother Samuel Hanson to George Wasington to provide the troops with shoes. Hanson, as President, ordered all foreign troops off American soil, as well as the removal of all foreign flags. This was quite the feat, considering the fact that so many European countries had a stake in the United States since the days following Columbus.

Hanson established the Great Seal of the United States, which all Presidents have since been required to use on all official documents.

President Hanson also established the first Treasury Department, the first Secretary of War, and the first

Foreign Affairs Department. Lastly, he declared that the fourth Thursday of every November was to be Thanksgiving Day, which is still true today.

The Articles of Confederation only allowed a President to serve a one year term during any three year period, so Hanson actually accomplished quite a bit in such little time.

Six other presidents were elected after him – Elias Boudinot (1783), Thomas Mifflin (1784), Richard Henry Lee (1785), Nathan Gorman (1786), Arthur St. Clair (1787), and Cyrus Griffin (1788) – all prior to Washington taking office.

So what happened?

Why don't we ever hear about the first seven Presidents of the United States?

It's quite simple – The Articles

of Confederation didn't work well. The individual states had too much power and nothing could be agreed upon.

A new doctrine needed to be written – something we know as the Constitution.

And that leads us to the end of our story.

George Washington was definitely not the first President of the United States. He was the first President of the United States under the Constitution we follow today.

And the first seven Presidents are forgotten in history."

We have dwelt long enough with this mountain (government), and if you haven't conformed to its ways and its laws, then you surely have felt the pain that she created for you. Over four hundred years of pain that Almighty Allah Himself allowed for us to endure.

Prophecy is not, until it happens; it is written hundreds of years in advance, and until the prophecy is fulfilled it cannot be applied to any time or place. Once even part of it is fulfilled then it entails the rest. Whether it be scripture or not, we are in the book and we are repeating the book. Things are revealed to us by our Creator, and He reveals it to us often, repeatedly, through signs (*ayahs*) of scripture or nature and symbols of art (natural or human representation). This is now the time (our time) to bring about that which He intends for this land. The land has become what it is because of its destiny; we are where we're supposed to be at the exact moment when we are there, it is prophecy. This country is no longer...—Babylon the great, for she has fallen.

Explicit Lyrics

I pray that all of you who hate the idea of a certain race of people striving for their independent economy, freedom, justice, and equality start understanding why! And at the price, we really shouldn't have to pay. All those who do seem to want us dead. Others also hated us for that...

Fuck you, Amerikay, kay, kay... United Snakes.

In God, you claim to trust; in you, I aim to hate.

Up yours with a big-ass butcher's knife,

And off with your head, you and your satanic wife.

You lie and steal, you hand out false wishes,

You cheat and kill with the help of your bitches:

Your presidents, the Clintons, the two burning Bushes,

Using house niggas to wash your dirty dishes.

Cancerous Colin and that bitch of the minute Rice,

Uncle Toms, Clarence Carters, and Jessie for the right price.

Sounds personal? No, this here is prophecy,

It would be best if you studied instead of going around so blindly.

Open your eyes and look at your history,

How you claimed equality and for us to be free.

Look in the mirror and see, if you can see,

You, carrying her flag and her iniquities.

If so, don't laugh and don't look at me;

Just prepare for the eternal flaming sea.

Fuck you, Amerikay, kay, kay, and all your allies.

Barack Obama, you are now being tried.

The cabinet that you chose and are tied to—

If you submit to her, you'll wish you had died.

She is all in the Motherland, killing its pride,

Its mosques and churches are the valid reasons she hides.

While you say nothing, knowing her sinister side,

Just wait, I wait, and conscious, I know mine.

Truth is In The Art V

The Creator is in the details—

The One God, the DNA,

Of Abraham, Isaac, and Israel,

Islam till this very day.

Ten Commandments, our instructions,

From the start, He said obey Me.

Then Eden's forbidden condition

Changed Adam's state of felicity.

That time until the ark,

Darkness had grown too deep.

Ignorance then plays its part

Of a world through water to weep.

Allah's plan vs. man's free will,

But safety through His covenant:

If not, then hell would fill,

And overflow in an instant.

The next ingredient was Christ:
The Law was taken in vain.
A new spiritual man's insight

Caused the world to go insane.

Like every grain of sand

And all that makes the Universe

Uniquely going hand in hand

It is just as important as the first.

These are the last of days;

Everything is to be complete.

The last Prophet and final plays,

Amen, now wait and see.

Look between the lines.

And try to see your part.

Poetry and writing are mine.

Truth is in the art.

5
Thy Kingdom Come

Our Father which art in heaven, Hallowed be thy name.
Thy kingdom come, Thy will be
done in earth, as it is in heaven.
Give us this day our daily bread.
And forgive us our debts, as we forgive our debtors.
And lead us not into temptation, but deliver
us from evil: For thine is the kingdom, and the
power, and the glory, forever. Amen.

If we were told things from the beginning exactly as we thought they were to be told to us, without parables, allegories, and mysteries, then many more of our prophets, leaders, and teachers would have died at the hands of these secret societies and their devils who rule the world today. They planned their dark deeds and are now being forced out into the light; how can the kingdom of heaven on earth come about with men marrying men, women marrying women, and priests raping little boys? How can nations oppress other nations and people, and how can they disregard the laws and commands of Allah and then claim to be doing His will?

Don't get it twisted, His will shall be done, but not in any way that could be imagined by anyone other than Him and whom He chooses. The Torah (Books of Moses), the Injil (Book of Revelation) and the Noble Qu'ran have foretold this and it shall be, Amen.

In that hour Jesus rejoiced in

*spirit, and said, I thank thee, O Father, Lord of heaven and earth, that thou hast hid these things from the **wise and prudent**, and hast revealed them unto babes: even so, Father; for so it seemed good in thy sight.*

Did you know that America (the world) thrives off of sickness and death? But the irony of it is that the sickness and the death permeates through the whole damn system, from the bottom up. She (America) uses and manipulates the lowest part (the ghettos and slums) to feed and enrich the wealthy. Case in point: Physical slavery was the mechanism used in previous years to set up the causes that affect these present days. What parallels that? Minimum wage, drugs, poor education, and so on. All of this leads to jails and institutions, and places like these are what breed the essence of sickness (sick humanity).

In most jails, food has been replaced with the worst kinds of substitutes and the inmates are being used as guinea pigs. They eat mostly soy products and over or undercooked pasta, little or no fruit, and vegetables that should be considered garbage. There are no vitamins on the commissary menu, even though it advertises them. The commissary menu prices are much higher than the public prices. If you get sick, there seems to be a waiting game. The air conditioning is on in the winter and the heat is on in the summer.

The revenue that is used to keep these

places running comes from you: the public and your taxes. Most of these places are owned by private citizens: politicians, judges, and prosecutors. They allow for the worst things possible to be used to sustain the death that these places produce. I'm just saying...

The initial stage of these places is the county jails that are supported by CECs (community educational centers). These places are used when the county jails and prisons become overcrowded. Most inmates live in CECs for at least six months and can stay for years if they can't make bail. Meanwhile, the jails and institutions get paid thousands of dollars per month for each inmate. Public defenders (pretenders), prosecutors, and judges know that most of the cases will not make it to trial and if they do, then it would cost too much money to convict someone for such petty crimes, so they keep you, the taxpayer, blindly paying for useless cases and housing petty criminals. All of this is done at the same time as to deceive the petty criminal to plea bargain to a sentence that exceeds his/her crime. The members of the grand jury are either wicked or naïve, because they are the people who indict, whether there is enough evidence or not, to keep the money coming into the institutions that they have investments in. The system must keep the jails overcrowded. Cops will arrest racially profiled Blacks (mostly) for any means necessary and if you don't have sufficient funds, then you are simply sh-t out of luck. Even if it is clear that you are innocent, the people who run the system will keep you incarcerated for as long as they can, and if you don't try to do something on your own to get out, they will keep you even longer.

These places are run by the real criminals—i.e. business owners, correctional officers, wardens, and so on. They steal, harass, oppress, kill and rape...whatever. These are the very ones who just don't get caught, and if they do, their actions are simply covered up by their peers. The real criminals are on Wall Street, stealing millions and billions, and are paying their way out of jail time. The real criminal is the world; it worships and praises these actions by way of propaganda: television, radio, advertising, etc. It allows its government to continue its anarchy by covering its eyes, ears, and mouth. Nothing is done to the crooked politicians, and if you have money, then it's your fight against justice.

All of this breeds into the jails the product of our sick minds, the world produces the madness (violence, sex, terror), and the government regulates and allows its reproduction. The crazy thing about it, is that because of this, it brings about the very reason there are disease, pollution, and hatred, anything that you can think of that causes the types of sickness that exist today.

When you look at the laws and how contrary the government is to them, you should be able to see the head of Satan emanating from the situation. America (the people) are just as guilty as the government. Even though its history defines who she is in a distorted kind of way, the people know that the government has always been deceitful, cunning, wicked, and oppressive of all she has come in contact with. Until the people come together and change the government, the people are the government.

If there are good people trying to do the right thing and they know of the bad people in their midst doing evil and don't expose them, they are part of the evil, because they are part of the whole. This is true with everything: family, friends, community, and government. The only way to set things right is to clean up the world and reeducate toward what is right and what is wrong:

> *Son of man, I have made you a watchman for the house of Israel; so hear the word I speak and give them warning from me. When I say to the wicked, 'O*

—
E
z
e
ki
el
3
3:
7
—
9

In the whole of existence, there has never been a time like this until now. There was a time when things were created, a time when things were prophesied. There was a time when things were revealed, and there will be a time when the days of this time will be healed. This time is a special time, however: the last hour. Adam had his time; Noah had his time; and Abraham, Moses, David, Solomon, and Jesus all had their times.

This is a special time. The time that all of the previous prophets came for was the time that we are in now:

> *And other sheep I have, which are not of this **fold**: them also I must bring, and they shall hear my voice; and there shall be one **fold**, and one shepherd.*

It is now Muhammad's time; it is our time, your time, depending on who you are. We are the fold that establishes the kingdom of heaven here on earth. We are the product of all of the above. We are the reason that all of the previous prophets had their time. In the previous times until now, our minds have been cloudy, from Adam and Eve's disobedience because of Satan's deceit:

The man said, "The
woman you put here
with me— she gave
me some fruit from
the tree, and I ate it."
Then the LORD God said to the
woman, "What is this you have
done?"
The woman said, "The serpent deceived
me, and I ate."
So the LORD God said to the
serpent, "Because you have
done this,
"Cursed
are you
above all
the
livestock
and all the
wild
animals!
You will crawl on your belly

a
n
d
y
o
u
w
i
l
l
e
a
t
d
u
s
t
a
l
l
t
h
e

d
a
y
s

o
f

y
o
u
r

l
i
f
e
.

A
n
d

I
w
i
l
l

p

u
t
e
n
m
i
t
y
between you and the woman,
and between your
offspring (or
seed) and hers;
he will crush (or
strike) your head,
and you will strike his heel."

—
Ge
nes
is
3:1
2–
15

Yes, Satan has a seed (mental offspring), and since that time, the two seeds have been grafting into each other. This was during the new beginning of Noah's time that there was a certain covenant between Allah and man.

When men began to increase in number on the earth and daughters were born to them, the sons of God saw that the daughters of men were beautiful, and they married any of them they chose. Then the LORD said, "My Spirit will not contend with man forever, for he is mortal; his days will be a hundred and twenty years."

Then God said to Noah and to his sons with him: "I now establish my covenant with you and with your descendants after you and with every living creature that was with you—the birds, the livestock and all the wild animals, all those that came out of the ark with you—every living creature on earth. I establish my covenant with you: Never again will all life be cut off by the waters of a flood; never again will there be a flood to destroy the earth."

And God said, "This is the sign of the covenant I am making between me and you and every living creature with you, a covenant for all generations to come: I have set my rainbow in the clouds, and it will be the sign of the covenant between me and the earth. Whenever I bring clouds over the earth and the

*rainbow appears in the clouds, I
will remember my covenant*

213

between me and you and all living creatures of every kind. Never again will the waters become a flood to destroy all life. Whenever the rainbow appears in the clouds, I will see it and remember the everlasting covenant between God and all living creatures of every kind on the earth."

— Genesis 9:8–12

Noah's time was to mark a new beginning for mankind: one language or speech, one way of life (religion, not culture) for one people. It was to mark this time in their time, but it wasn't for them in their time to accomplish this, so their language was confused and they were scattered over all of the earth:

> *Now the whole world had one language and a common speech. As men moved eastward, they found a plain in Shinar and settled there.*
>
> *They said to each other, "Come, let's make bricks and bake them thoroughly." They used brick instead of stone, and tar for mortar. Then they said, "Come, let us build ourselves a city, with a tower that reaches to the heavens, so that we may make a name for ourselves and not be scattered over the face of the whole earth."*
>
> *But the LORD came down to see the city and the tower that the men were building. The LORD said, "If as one people speaking the same language they have begun to do this, then nothing they plan to do will be impossible*

for them. Come, let us go down and confuse their language so they will not understand each other."

So the LORD scattered them from there over all the earth, and they stopped building the city. That is why it was called Babel —because there the LORD confused the language of the whole world. From there the LORD scattered them over the face of the whole earth.

Abraham was the one whom Allah

established His friendship and His covenant
through for all of mankind, and out of him
was to issue forth the

exact same message that Allah witnessed of Adam, and that was to permeate from and through all of the prophets: one G-d (Allah)! Abraham's first son was Ishmael through Hagar, his second wife, who was given to him by his first wife, Sarah "to be his wife." Sarah at the time could not conceive. When it was time for her to conceive, she laughed, and then she lied, so the Bible says:

> *Then the LORD said to Abraham, "Why did Sarah laugh and say, 'Will I really have a child, now that I am old?' Is anything too hard for the LORD? I will return to you at the appointed time next year and Sarah will have a son."*
>
> *Sarah was afraid, so she lied and said, "I did not laugh." But he said, "Yes, you did laugh."*

—
Gen
esis
18:1
3—

It was through Sarah that Christianity and Judaism came, by way of Isaac, Jacob (Israel) and Moses, David, and Jesus. Her lack of faith, on top of her denial when questioned, might have caused a ripple effect, bringing about the retardation of these two religions (immoral sexualities and adulteries of Allah unchallenged and defended by the people and their government).

In all of this, mankind had to deal with Satan's seed that was grafted into its own with the thought of destroying mankind. During this time, there could be no better way to reveal things to man except by way of prophecy. To tell man outright was to also reveal this information to Satan and to aid Satan in the destruction of man. So came the significance of Moses and of Jesus during their times: Moses' time was for a literal (physical) message, and Jesus' time was more of a spiritual (emotional) message.

> *And other sheep I have, which are not of this **fold**: them also I must bring, and they shall hear*

my voice; and there shall be one **fold**, *and one shepherd.*

Ishmael was the one whom all of the focus was intentionally taken off of. This was done either by the grafted seed of man being confused because of the obvious, or/and it was done by Allah Himself, for His plan. Through

Ishmael came the only prophet like Moses, Prophet Muhammad:

> *The LORD your God will raise up for you a **prophet like me** from among your own brothers. You must listen to him. For this is what you asked of the LORD your God at Horeb on the day of the assembly when you said, "Let us not hear the voice of the LORD our God nor see this great fire anymore, or we will die." The LORD said to me: "What they say is good. **I will raise** up for them **a prophet like you** from among their brothers; **I will put my words in his mouth**, and **he will tell them everything I command him**. If anyone does not listen to my words that the prophet speaks in my name, I myself will call him to account. But a prophet who presumes to speak in my name anything I have not commanded him to say, or a prophet who speaks in the name*

of other gods, must be put to death."

You may say to yourselves, "How can we know when a message has not been spoken by the LORD ?"

*If what a prophet proclaims **in the name of the LORD** does not take place or come true, that is a message the LORD has not spoken. That prophet has spoken presumptuously. Do not be afraid of him.*

—

Deuteronomy 18:15–22

He is the reason for the creation of all of mankind, the answer to the problem of the grafted seeds. It is during this time that man is to be healed and the kingdom of heaven is to be established. He is the reason of the wars and the rumors of wars; He is the one. Allah reveals things to man often with His signs and His symbols, His revelations, and prophecies through His prophets and chosen people. The symmetrical thread in all of their messages confirms that it is time.

Many give praises to people and they immortalize the dead. They find glorification in material things and spend in excess on the production of vanity. They discard the message of the prophets and worship them as gods. They alter the books of G-d and change His laws to fit their own lust and desires. Witness the fact that I follow the teachings of the prophets and I honor them for the message they brought to humanity. They are my heroes and because of their message I place myself in harm's way in order to reach out to my family first and then to my friends, enemies, the world.

Truth Is In The Art VI

He is in the life's force,

The breath, inside the blood,

In you, of the original source,

The proof of all that's good.

Like the IRS's "Reign of Error,"

Slavery was their goal,

By deleting history with terror,

And kill the Black man's soul.

But the lessons they cannot hide,

Four hundred years of murder,

Takes away all of their pride.

Let's look at the bigger picture.

The house built by the slaves,

Never had it any intent,

Would die and go to their graves,

Then, have a Black president.

"Behold a pale horse,"

And who is its rider?

The man of perdition, of course,

He couldn't get any brighter.

Government from the caucus mountain,

Come out of her, my people;

Abundance is your fountain;

It makes you more than equal.

Actions prove who you are,

And history proves your worth;

Blood on your hands thus far.

Wash them of their curse.

Look between the lines,

Try to see your part.

Poetry and writing are mine.

Truth is in the art.

6
Pain and Joy

When he opened the fifth seal, I saw under the altar the souls of those who had been slain because of the word of God and the testimony they had maintained. They called out in a loud voice, "How long, Sovereign Lord, holy and true, until you judge the inhabitants of the earth and avenge our blood?" Then each of them was given a white robe, and they were told to wait a little longer, until the number of their fellow servants and brothers who were to be killed as they had been was completed.

To the woman he said,
"I will greatly
increase your pains in
childbearing; with
pain you will give
birth to children.
Your
desire
will be
for your
husband,
and he
will rule
over
you."
To Adam he said, "Because you listened to
your wife and ate from the tree about which I
commanded you,

'You must not eat of it,'
"Cursed is
the
ground
because
of you;
through
painful
toil you
will eat of
it all the
days of
your life.

— Genesis 3:16

In 1993, one day in October was the most painful day in my entire life. Since then, there has been no one to talk to or even to confide in concerning the most depressing times in my life: the drug use, my failures, hard times, and so on.

The pain of a brother and sister who didn't and don't understand me and who wrote me off to die as if I don't even exist, the pain of other relatives who didn't and don't understand the reality of life and its gravitational pull affecting how one perceives the truth of this (Satan's) world.

The pain of being deceived concerning whom and how to worship, placing Jesus on a level with Allah and then confusing you with the spirit of a trinity, making Jesus out to be divine, a son, and then to be one and the same as Allah, changing his color from original to pale and having you worship his mother as the mother of God.

The pain of deception so they can rule the world and enslave the masses physically, mentally, emotionally, economically, and spiritually...

Epistle:

To: Her & Him What's up?

I was and still am your brother, and I had a problem. However, I have always noticed that if it were anyone else, you would have helped them. I tried to reach out, but your hearts were hardened. Don't get me wrong because I don't blame you. I would have backed off from me too, but the difference is, I wouldn't have given up on either of you. I just couldn't see past the world's glitter and gold. I saw it when we were young, and I guess that is the part that really hurt. But there is good in this world and good in the Hereafter; you don't have to sell your souls to gain material wealth. I was the talk of the family, friends, and selves. But you know what; I'd rather have my spiritual wealth and health. Open your eyes and see, I'm not bad even though now you don't know me, just some mistakes I had to make in order to reach where I am now. I was and am your brother, the one who cared. The way you all looked at me, if the tide were turned, I couldn't. That was harsh judgment. My life was written as well as yours and everyone else's, from the beginning. "How do you judge?" You would give a stranger help before helping your own brother. I know my confusion couldn't help you see, but like I said, "situation reversed, I'd have never given up on either of you." I was always proud to see your successes and always hoped for you two to excel. Trying to beat life was the way. I know now if I hadn't tried this I wouldn't know how. I've studied and now shown myself approved, proven all things necessary that Islam is really the one and only truth.

With Love, Your Brother, Raheem

P.S. If I die before I wake in this
world again, trust and believe
on the other side, with grace
and mercy I'll win.

When your life is painful, it can create many emotions. There can be depression, and it can take you to the point of even wanting to die or to hurt yourself or others, but what keeps you from doing this on the conscious level is desire, though sometimes on the subconscious level you find different reasons to fail. With the help of society, peer pressure, and family neglect, the use of drugs tends to become fair to the individual.

What the world doesn't know is that the person who succumbs to this type of action is hurting in so many ways that it can't simply be explained. It might even go back to their childhood, maybe even to the point of being physiologically induced through abuse. What is true is that to bring this person back to the surface, a quickening must occur. A deep desire in that person must be awakened, and sometimes, Allah forbid, it takes a certain type of tragedy in that person's life to cause an upward spike or downward spiral.

If one has a strong spiritual relationship with his or her Creator, eventually, destiny calls him or her and the person is safe. At the same time, family support is a vital key; if there is no family support, then the spiritual relationship with The Creator must then be extremely strong or there is no hope.

Shall a Man Rob God?

Once upon a time not so long ago, a man got caught up in the snares of drugs. This man claimed to be Muslim, but the drugs possessed him and he was oh so much other than himself, living the life of a jinn. It didn't matter how hard he tried to let the drugs go and no matter how he tried to reach out to his family, he had no one to help him...so he thought. He sought out companionship in his lonely world and tried to live amongst Muslims, but he kept his secret life to himself. Thinking that he could control his habit and eventually quit, he continued living with this vice discreetly. Then one day he went on a binge, getting high off of money he had made or stolen, and he found himself in the mosque, all alone, and stole from God. That man later repented. Even though it took some time to do this because of the addiction, through his patience and constancy, God finally healed him.

Once upon a time every day in life, a child starves to death, a homeless man dies in the streets, the sick and the elderly are abandoned, but still the people go off to work, they go home, they go to church. If they give their tithes and offerings, those go into the preachers' pockets and the preachers buy fancy cars, homes, and lifestyles. Instead of doing the right thing with their money, the world spend money on sporting events, extravagant entertainment, and useless activities though the world and its people are suffering. There are billion-dollar stadiums, trillion-dollar wars, and excessive salaries given to so many people that it throws off the balance that is due to the world. And there are so-called normal people acting as if there is nothing wrong...daily, as if all is well. Still, children starve to death, the homeless die in the streets, and the elderly are abandoned. Shall a man rob God? Love God with all your heart, mind, and soul. And love your neighbor as you love yourself." I say again, "Shall a man rob God?"

United Snakes Of America

So much knowledge on the planet,

But the right people don't even want it.

They just sit at home in the darkness,

Fronting on all that they can get,

While many others miss happiness.

The truth of it all right in place:

A dragon, the serpent, a bunch of snakes,

Feeding on the people like a beast.

When will it end, or will they wake?

Only Allah knows the end of her feast.

Behold a pale horse yells the Gospel,

A hint in the book that they hold.

Really contains many for the able,

Even after that book was sold.

"In G-d we trust"? Some real sh-t,

Because actions are the actual testimony.

Ruled by a cruel son of a bitch,

And controlled by a group so horny.

Commandments disregarded, thrown way down,

His laws are in reverse; what a shame.

Everything is the opposite in every town;

Dog in their language is his name.

This new country is in absolute havoc,

Policing the world with democracy (hypocrisy),

Its people are immune to the shock,

Its motto is "Be all you can be."

In the end, the Revelation revealed,

Dictatorship from the Most High Allah.

Sins of this world then will be sealed.

No more Hitler's, Bushes, or Nimrods.

The Torah, the Gospel, and the Qu'ran,

Manifested all this world needed.

If only the people kept their bond,

Eternal paradise could be granted.

Words hurt those who do not understand.

They burn all the high places,

Setting right the wrong and stinging,

Except the pious and the chaste.

Wake up to all that is killing you.

The deceit of slavery and disease,

Aids, drugs, all nothing new.

Study, I beg; study, I plead.

Poor health care and no jobs.

Rightly, there should be no more war.

Take it all back, be the mob.

Be backed by the Lord, and soar.

Turn away and return to the origin,

Submit your total submission.

Turn off iniquity and all of your sins,

Totally away from the temptation.

He gave us scriptures, ayahs, and verses,

To help you sort out the truth.

Instead of guns, hospitals, and hearses,

That keeps you from establishing the new—

The new, all you can't imagine,

Eyes haven't seen nor ears heard.

Coming in the end for whoever wins,

This race back home, even the nerd.

Homosexuals, fastest-growing to date

It's so unnatural and a real shame.

Talk against it, and they say you hate,

Because it is the pride of their game.

An abomination unto Allah's very sight,

Evolving from the sickness of the world.

Look at it; look at their plight.

Vice versa, the boy wants to be a girl.

Of this, nothing produced will stand,

Because life wasn't created for it.

A woman, a woman, a man, a man

Producing offspring, leading to bliss.

All that these snakes permit and do,

It is against the One and the True.

It's not complicated. And nothing is new.

To change the red to black to blue,

The all in all, the wrong in you,

It is inside your mind, the Clue.

Open your eyes, look at America,

Depending on your position, say, "Yes, Sah."

The real dragon is the Massah,

Slave owner, killer, so-called ruler—

Shaytan is in high places, the murderer.

But your term is over, America.

The Middle Passage, Tuskegee, Jena six, Katrina,

Black Wall Street, Alabama, Martin Luther King,

AIDS, drugs, gangs, poverty, Texas, unemployment,

Health care, education, racism, Malcolm X,

The Black Panther Party, Cuba, Iraq, Afghanistan,

Israel, Rosewood—is that enough secrets of the Ku Klux Klan?

How does it feel to be an absolute fool,

Ignoring the truth just to be cool,

Knowing that the scriptures are reality's tool?

To overlook invites the flaming pool,

Eternal hell, Bush sitting on the stool

And bitch of the minute Rice, the fuel.

Cancerous Colin, will he be saved,

Or are the Caucasians in black skin today?

Will you, or did you pave your way?

It won't matter on judgment day.

In front of your Lord, what will you say?

"I, Ah, well, see..." Never mind, burn and stay.

Those are the writings, "Oh, say can you see!?"

A warning to those, a simple plea,

For the hidden secrets of this country,

To let loose its burden, set them free.

Or feel the wrath of your destiny,

That, that is, was and forever will be.

Verse Of The Throne

Allah, there is no god but He, the Living, the Eternal. Neither
slumber nor sleep seizes Him. To Him belongs what is in the
heavens and in the earth. Who can intercede with Him, except by
His permission? He knows what lies before them and after them
and they know nothing of his knowledge, save such as He wills. His
throne encompasses the heavens and the earth and He never
wearies of preserving them. He is Sublime, the Exalted.

Qur'an 2:255

Truth is In The Art VII

Life is in the mind of us,

Coming from a glorious thought:

It's time...and now to trust

His word and what He's taught.

The evolution of the pen,

The knowledge from teachers,

A combination of all the men

Putting thought into computers.

One man alone is nothing,

Even all of us today,

Without the beginning,

The past would have to stay.

From Him, we all came,

To Him, we shall return;

If that isn't of the sum,

It's another chance to learn.

Dying is anything but new.

In God, we live and will die,

And now we're born again,

To show Him that we tried.

The truth is in the art,

The Art of Life and Death,

And if death do us part,

May these words pass the test.

Our mission is to evolve

Past those material things,

It also is to solve

Why do we not have wings?

Look between the lines.

And try to see your part.

Poetry and writing are mine.

Truth is in the art.

7
Joy and Pain

And (remember) when your Lord said to the angels: "I am going to create a man (Adam) from sounding clay of altered black smooth mud.

"So, when I have fashioned him completely and breathed into him (Adam) the soul which I created for him, then fall (you) down prostrating yourselves unto him."

—
Noble Quran 15:28-2

And the Lord formed man of the dust of the ground, and breathed into his nostrils the breath of life; and man became a living being.

John 16:20

DNA

Roderick Williams died
***"Unless a man is born
again..."*** Raheem Abdul
Muslim Muhammad became
a living being. Before this I
was with Allah, (but I did not
know):
***"Before I formed
you in the womb, I
knew you"*** ***"Before
you were born I
sanctified you"***
I came from Allah
by way of my
father's loins, I
bear witness of
my Creator
because He is.
Whose genetic

makeup is
anything like
mine?
In His breath I was created,
and there is none other like
me. My fingerprints have
never been, nor shall they
ever be. The hurt and pain
that I feel,
The long suffering
caused by my
incarceration, The
death of my
mother and
father,
My experiences through the obstacles of life
produced by my open enemy— Together
these things are who I am.
Out of nothing I was created:
A little
bit of
this, a
little bit
of that,

From
the
dust of
the
earth,
A nucleic acid molecule in the
shape of a twisted double
strand. Double helix that is the
major component of
chromosomes
And carries genetic information
which is found in all living things.
Reproduces itself,
Is the means by which hereditary
characteristics pass from one generation to
the next.

DNA

Fire burns the dross from
gold and makes pure refined
gold. Centuries of pressure
turn coal into diamonds.
Out of darkness comes the light.
Trials and afflictions are what truly define
a man.
And the pain in life causes one

to think, dis

cover, and create. —Raheem M

How can one survive the mission that brings grief to him if he has no one to help him through it? It is just not possible; one cannot. If one is created to be destined to live and/or die for a cause and all of one's life is made of pain and sorrow, there must be a driving force to keep him motivated and focused. Thus, one is totally dependent on a higher power—i.e., his Creator —but only if he is not derelict of his duty or running away from his responsibility will his Creator be pleased with that one and grant him joy (happiness).

This is what drives a man; it is the joy of his life when all else seems lost and darkness surrounds him, from the depths of his soul is the light that his Creator placed there to remind and re-inspire him in this world—the tangible part of himself, the perfect whole of his very being, his completeness, his soul mate, his oneness, his woman: his wife.

She is who helps and reminds him of his goal, keeps him focused on it, and consoles him in the pain of it, so she must be cultivated in a way to assure her of how he feels. This process cannot be false or even misleading; it must be natural and real. His feelings cannot be infatuation or lust. No matter how it begins, the end result is that they must, without any doubt at all, be true and unadulterated love.

What Did Prophet Jesus Really Teach

Jesus (Isa)(as) Said

"Don't worship me, worship Allah"
        Bible.

"I could do nothing, except of Him that sent me"

Bible.

"I am among your brothers, the prophets"
            Bible.

"Never could I do what I had no right to do"
            Quran.

"I am the son of man"

Bible.

"I didn't come to change the law, only to fulfill the law"

Bible.

"You know what is in my heart, though I know not what is in
yours"   Quran.

"Those who call themselves Jews and are not"
            Bible.

257

"Worship Allah, my Lord and yours"

        Bible.

"Our Creator which art in Heaven"

        Bible.

"Not my will, but let Thy will be done"

        Bible.

"The things I do, you'll do greater"

        Bible.

"If I don't go, the Comforter (Muhammad) shall not come unto you"   Bible.

"Forgive them, Lord, for they know not what they do"

        Bible.

"There where I am you may be also"

        Bible.

From Allah (God), we all came, and to Him, we all shall return. Allah (G-d) has no sons nor daughters nor mother or father. There is no one and nothing comparable or equal to Him, and no one and nothing has the right to be worshiped but Him. The tri-headed god, what the world declares as the trinity, is the main thought or process of thinking that defies the first commandment:

"Worship Me and Me alone for I am a jealous God that will visit the iniquity upon the fathers even unto the sons up to the fourth and fifth generations of them."

Truth is In The Art VIII

Art is in our minds;

Learning is what we do.,

Lord help us to find,

Answers revealing Your truth.

Hijrah,; a western Muslim's mind,

Divine light changing its course;

It wasn't hard to find,

It is simply a matter of choice:

Open your eyes and see,

What all the Prophets told:

The truth shall make you free,

On it, stand up bold!

For what's a man to do?

How can you even live?

If what you have is untrue,

There's nothing for you to give.

This life force is your gift,

To only it you owe,

Don't fall through the sift,

For lack of what you know.

Study and prove this wrong;

If so, it will dissipate,

But, if it shall not be gone,

Catch up and don't be late.

The vineyard time is now,

The Householders' fruits are ripe,

The Cornerstone is in town,

The Ka'bah is in sight.

Look between the lines,

And try to see your part.,

Poetry and writing are mine.,

Truth is in the art.

8
Sellout

What happened to the backbone of the Black race? Where are the Malcolm's, the Kings, the Moses's, and Christs, and why are we turning inward on ourselves with unparalleled violence? At the same time, we're ignoring what's happening to our race, and most of us are selling out or have sold out to the lifestyle of the Dragon. Who are you? What are you? Are you a **SELLOUT**? Have you betrayed your race? A sellout is "a person who betrays something or someone to which he or she is said to owe allegiance," according to the Oxford English Dictionary, Selling out means "to betray a person or cause for gain."

Jesus Predicts His Betrayal

"I am not referring to all of you; I know those I have chosen. But this is to fulfill the scripture: 'He who shares my bread has lifted up his heel against me.'

"I am telling you now before it happens, so that when it does happen you will believe that I am He. I tell you the truth, whoever accepts anyone I send accepts me; and whoever accepts me accepts the one who sent me."

*After he had said this, Jesus was troubled in spirit and testified, "I tell you the truth, one of you is going to **betray** me."*

His disciples stared at one another, at a loss to know which of them he meant. One of them, the disciple whom Jesus loved, was reclining next to him. Simon Peter motioned to this disciple and said, "Ask him which one he means."

Leaning back against Jesus, he asked him, "Lord, who is it?"

Jesus answered, "It is the one to whom I will give this piece of bread when I have dipped it in the dish." Then, dipping the piece of bread, he gave it to Judas Iscariot, son of Simon. As soon as Judas took the bread, Satan entered into him.

— John 13:18-27

A well known author, Randall Kennedy, has a book out titled *Sellout* that helps to shed some light on whether or not the shoe fits the person according to his view on the subject.

Some gangs and rappers, leaders and teachers—anyone in any position that touches our people in any kind of way whatsoever—who partake in the violence are in one way or another sellouts. Whether it is by entertainment propaganda or any type of influence, how can you advertise products on communicable devices and help target your own people to be trapped into a web of debt—i.e., Rent to Own. Magic Johnson, I hope you can at least act like you didn't know. That's just a small example of how some of us sell out. Though our actions can very well be innocent, we all need to reevaluate what we are doing and whom we pledge our allegiance to.

Then there is the extreme sellout. Point in case: A Black gang targets Black women to be killed, during the month of October as a means of gang initiation. I simply have one question for that one: Who in the hell have they *sold out* to? I guess we can say that the gain in this type of selling out comes from the bloody money or positions that they hold. Another question is, Who is the bigger sellout—them, or us, because we sit back and talk about it and do nothing? Have we forgotten that these gang members are/were our children? They have placed the value of colors and things above the value of life. The most precious thing that Allah gave us is life, and we have devalued it to where it's worth is about a dollar and twenty-five cents—some places a little more, and some a little less. Some rappers add to this type of selling out by feeding the fire of these actions because they make their music with these types of lyrics only because this is the only type of music that they can sell; therefore, they betray their people and their people's causes for gain—perpetual, murderous, negative, and satanic gain: And we promote it by giving it our stamp of approval, making movies for profit instead of for help.

There is more negative influence in the Black communities than there is positive, and it seems as if we are our own worst enemy now, because the voices opposing or speaking out against the violence and injustice to Black people is almost unheard now. I love people like anyone who stands up and speak against the people that are getting away with murdering and misusing —not just Black people, but any people that these things are happening to— people like Minister Louis Farrakhan and Reverend Al Sharpton—hell, if Pee-wee Herman stood up for us, I'd learn to love him, too.

We have more than enough on our plate with an open enemy that Allah revealed to us. This enemy is at the root of the cause of the hurt and pain that we are now inflicting on and administering to ourselves. I plead to those whom Allah has given eyes to see, ears to hear, and tongues to speak with to stand up and fight for the rights that have been stolen from us as a race of people. We do not need terror to use as a weapon, or any kind of violence whatsoever. The only things we need are true faith and actions to prove our faith. The only person we need is our one and true Creator, who, by now, we should have proven to ourselves is the Originator of the heavens and the earth, the seen and the unseen, and His name is not a name that can even be reversed, His name is Allah.

The stories in the Bible are stories of our ancestors, yet we continue to spiral downwards and at the same time backwards with the illusion as if we have truly arrived wherever we were going, along with our slave master. The reality, whether you can see it now or not, is that the slave master's term has come to its end and Allah (God) wants to show this to the whole world. He reveals knowledge to whom He pleases, and He conceals knowledge from whom He pleases. The fruit is ripe and the time is nigh. Wake up, Israel, the Muslims of the Twelve Tribes, and gather with the Muslims of the Twelve Princes. It is time for the prayers of the righteous to be heard.

But what is the good of this world if we have lost our soul, misplaced our spirit and given up or sold out our will to strive toward what is right *by any means necessary?*

Satan has been ruling this world, and we have been following the sadistic insanity that his ruler ship has created, thinking that we have been doing what was right, because he has made us believe that the wrong is right and the right is wrong. We've been molded into that which fits the mold that our enemy, Satan, has made for us, and we have discarded (put aside) studying for the higher achievement, which is to study for the knowledge leading to the gift of eternal life. Once upon a time, we just accepted what was handed down to us by our parents and grandparents. During those times, it was the normal thing to do. Nowadays, things are different because they have been proven different and people choose based on understanding of the knowledge that they have acquired through the studying that they have done. There is a real pleasure now: the pleasure of worshipping the Only True and Living God (Allah).

Allah Is the Greatest

So no one misunderstands,

My intentions or what I do,

This book is my ultimate goal.

The Witness, the Warner, the Man,

Exposing to all that is true,

Despite this day's Pharaoh:

Turning my face to the Ka'bah,

Hoping Allah uses me to save,

In my heart blowing my trumpet,

"There is no other god, only Allah,"

And Muhammad is His slave,

The last and final Prophet:

Standing boldly on His word,

Challenging all those who oppose,

Allah alone is my protection.

If killed by the enemies enemy's sword,

And in case nobody knows,

A martyr is an instant salvation.

One day you will find out,

Why you were created,

And what you must do.

Today, I don't even doubt,

The reasons why I'm hated—-

Or loved—by all of you:

Simply taking a stand,

At a time when someone should,

And just giving; you the latest,:

Hoping that together we band,

Like only the Muslims could,

Knowing Allah is the Greatest.

Identity Crisis

A person's identity lies within his/her culture. The Afro-American culture is a hybrid culture that was created by Euro-Americans only by Allah's permission. In order to do this, they had to try to completely annihilate the African history of our people that was within the slaves brought here from Africa (William Lynch). A new race of people was created out of this process. As a product of this oppression and terror, it took me, on and off, forty-five years and counting to realize who I am. Because of my rebellious nature to this system, and because the system is directly and indirectly opposed to the laws of Allah, I could not and would not conform to it. Those of you who are deeply rooted in her and who cannot or will not come out of her ("come out of her, My people") will go down with her.

Because Barrack Obama is of African and Caucasian descent, he is indirectly ingrained into the slave situation; he is Black, therefore, he is of us. Now, pertaining to understanding our direct oppression caused from the William Lynch process of oppression, he is not. He is grafted into the oppression of Euro-

America and her secret societies and their ways of making a slave. But the question is, who is he? That is to be determined by what and how he does things as a Black man in the seat of president: his intentions and how he will help the downtrodden of America. The slave master needs no help in making a slave now; it's just that her system of ruler ship over the slave is over. Her once slave is waking up and becoming the true slave to who it belongs to: Allah.

Who we are is who Allah allowed for us to become. The oppression and affliction were pretty much necessary to create the personalities that we as Black people have today. They cause those who are chosen to have very deep spiritual entities. In turn, this causes a closer connection to Allah, if one submits his/her whole self to Him.

Barrack Hussain Obama is a Muslim name. Does he profess Christianity? Is he Catholic, Jewish? If so, we must consider who he really is.

His identity is rooted in himself, and it has not been cut off from his ancestors. On the other hand, all Afro-American roots have been severed. They know not who they are, especially as a people. That doesn't matter,

however; we are genetically coded to be risen back to our true selves. For example, though I am a product of slavery here in America, conditioned to be other than myself, I know now who I am: I am a descendent of Abraham through the lineage if Israel Jacob. In bondage for over four hundred years, my bloodline can be traced.

In the Qu'ran:

> *And [mention] when Abraham said, "My Lord, show me how You give life to the dead." [Allah] said, "Have you not believed?" He said, "Yes, but [I ask] only that my heart may be satisfied." [Allah] said, "Take four birds and commit them to yourself. Then [after slaughtering them] put on each hill a portion of them; then call them - they will come [flying] to you in haste. And know that Allah is Exalted in Might and Wise."*

ran 2:260

The question remains: Who are you?

Are we still in bondage? Some of us are. Are we still considered slaves? Yes and no. To be in bondage is to be tied down, restrained with no way of escape. To be a slave is to be subject to a master, having no choice in the matter, whether you are paid or not. You are controlled and regulated in a manner not fit for animals. Sometimes you are beaten by the police, broken, and many times killed. You are nothing but livestock, traded, raped, and abused. You endure the most hardship of any human being alive. So, yes, some of us are still slaves to a more sinister slave master, but his system is now failing him. Some of us are in bondage to a false identity: Caucasians in a Black man's body.

> *Do you then hope that they would believe in you, and a party from among them indeed used to hear the Word of Allah, then altered it after they had understood it, and they know (this).*
>
> *And when they meet those who believe they say: We*

believe, and when they are alone one with another they say: Do you talk to them of what Allah has disclosed to you that they may contend with you by this before your Lord? Do you not then understand?

Do they not know that Allah knows what they keep secret and what they make known?

And there are among them illiterates who know not the Book but only lies, and they do but conjecture. Woe, then, to those who write the book with their hands and then say: This is from Allah, so that they may take for it a small price; therefore woe to them for what their hands have written and woe to them for what they earn.

And they say: Fire shall not touch us but for a few days. Say: Have you received a

promise from Allah, then
Allah will not fail to perform
His promise, or do you speak
against Allah what you do
not know? Yea, whoever
earns evil and his sins beset
him on every side, these are
the

inmates of the fire; in it they shall abide.
And (as for) those who believe and do good deeds, these are the dwellers of the garden; in it they shall abide.

And when We made a covenant with the children of Israel: You shall not serve any but Allah and (you shall do) good to (your) parents, and to the near of kin and to the orphans and the needy, and you shall speak to men good words and keep up prayer and pay the poor-rate. Then you turned back except a few of you and (now too) you turn aside.

And when We made a covenant with you: You shall not shed your blood and you shall not turn your people out of your cities; then you gave a promise while you witnessed.

Yet you it is who slay your people and turn a party from

among you out of their homes, backing each other up against them unlawfully and exceeding the limits; and if they should come to you, as captives you would ransom them—while their very turning out was unlawful for you. Do you then believe in a part of the Book and disbelieve in the other? What then is the reward of such among you as do this but disgrace in the life of this world, and on the day of resurrection they shall be sent back to the most grievous chastisement, and Allah is not at all heedless of what you do.

These are they who buy the life of this world for the hereafter, so their chastisement shall not be lightened nor shall they be helped.

—Holy Qu'ran

Truth is In The Art IX

Look in between the lines.

And try to see your part.

Poetry and writing are mine.

Truth is in the art.

Oh, say, can you see

Secrets they tried to hide?

Do you think you're free?

Are those who have died?

This government is constitution-less;

It brags in God's name,

Terrorizing while it oppresses,

But you are who they blame.

You voted and are in charge?

Let it get out of hand?

And now you're living large.

But still won't take a stand.

How does it feel inside?

Oh, don't have a conscience?

Swelling up, or is it pride?

Is looking away contagious?

In the beginning, was the truth,

It was mixed up and destroyed,

Cream of utter, brand-new,

The truth still on top, annoyed?

And now, what will happen?

Do you really think you're saved?

Judgment day or entrapment,

You just let yourself get played.

It is in the flow of motion,

Through all the threads of time,

Twisted, turned, and even broken,

Resurrected and reversed in your mind.

Table of Contents
No table of contents entries found.

Who are you?

I am a Muslim. I am not a prefixed word before that. I am simply a Muslim, One who follows the Sunnah (teachings, ways, actions) of prophet Muhammad (SAW), and the righteous predecessors (ra). Prophet Muhammad (SAW) said to his followers: "Three generations after me and you will be of me no more." He (SAW) didn't lie; that has indeed happened. Now you have Sunni, Shiite, and more. That is the problem; we now have seventy-three sects of Muslims. There lies the division. Allah (SWT) says to the Prophet(SAW): "On this day have I perfected my favor upon you, completed your religion and give it the name Islam," and we were called Muslims. Why do we divide ourselves with all of these titles we place in front of the word Muslim? All of the prophets were Muslim, and we are Muslims even though we follow the ways and the sayings of Prophet Muhammad (SAW). We can settle our differences later, but for now, we must all consider ourselves to simply be Muslims first.

The Prophet (sallAllahu 'alayhi wa sallam) said:

"The Jews split into seventy-one sects; one will be in Paradise (i.e., those who followed Moses) and seventy will be in the Fire. The Christians split into seventy-two sects; seventy-one will be in the Fire and one will be in Paradise (i.e., those who followed Jesus). And by the One in Whose Hand is the soul of Muhammad, this Ummah (nation) of mine will split into seventy-three sects; one will be in Paradise and seventy-two will be in the Fire. It was asked, "Who are they, O Messenger of Allah?" He (peace be upon him) said, "Al-Jama'ah (i.e., the group which adheres steadfastly to the way of the Prophet, peace be upon him, and his Companions)." And in another narration:" (Those who follow) what I and my Companions are following."

[The hadeeth is Hasan and is reported by

at-Tirmidhee (no.

291

2643), Ibn Waddaah in al-Bid'ah (p. 85), al-Aajurree in ash-Sharee'ah (p. 15) and in al-Arba'een, al-Haakim (1/128-129), Ibn Nasr in as-Sunnah (no. 62), al-Laalikaa'ee in as-Sunnah (no. 147), Ibn al-Jawzee in Talbees Iblees (p. 16) and al-'Uqailee in ad-Du'afaa' (2/262) from the hadeeth of 'Abdullah ibn 'Amr (radhiAllahu 'anhu].

Furthermore, there are additional Ahadith to support the one above, such as:

"The best of people is my generation, then those who come after them, then those who come after them (i.e. the first three generations of Muslims)."

[Reported by Bukhari and Muslim.
Narrated 'Aisha (radhiAllahu 'anha), Shaykh Al Albaani declares it Hasan in Sahih

Al Jaami' no. 3288]

"The best of people are my generation, then the second, then the third, then there will come a people, having no good in them."

[Related by Abdullah ibn Mas'ood (radhiAllahu 'anhu) in Tabaraanee in Al-Kabeer, Shaykh Al Albaanee declares it to be Hasan. See Silsilatul Ahaadeeth ad-Da'eefah no. 3569, and Saheeh Al Jaami' no. 3293]

"The best of people are my generation, then those who follow after them, then those who follow after them, then there will come after them a people who will be fat, and they will love obesity, bearing witness before being asked to."

[Related by the Umars, sons of Husayn (radhiAllahu 'anhu), in Tirmidthee, authenticated by Imaam Al Haakim, Shaykh Al

*Albaanee declares it to be Saheeh.
See Silsilatul Ahaadeeth*

*AsSaheehah no. 699, and Saheeh Al Jaami'
no. 3294].*

And the Prophet (sallAllahu 'alayhi wa sallam) consistently indicated that those who are upon the Qur'an & Sunnah as per the understanding of the earliest generations of Muslims will be upon the truth.

"A group of my Ummah shall remain steadfast, on the truth, victorious, unharmed by those who oppose them, and do not support them, until death or until the Day of Resurrection."

[Al-Bukhaari, Book 71 no. 3641 Sahih Muslim, no. 1920]

"I left upon you two things of which you will never go astray after them: The Book of Allaah and my Sunnah. They will never be separated until they return to me at the Haud (the Pond)."

[Reported by   Al-Hakim,
*   Tirmidhi,   andAl-*

Albaanee has authenticated this hadeeth in Saheeh Al-Jaami']

To add more, as is apparent in the Sunnah, the Prophet (sallAllahu 'alayhi wa sallam) disassociated himself from those who corrupt his Sunnah and gives glad tidings of Paradise to those who uphold it:

The Prophet (may Allah be pleased with him) said, "He who turns away from my Sunnah is not from me."

[Reported by al-Bukhaaree (Eng. trans. 7/1-2, no. l), Muslim (Eng. Trans. 2/703, no. 3236) and An-Nasaa'ee]

Abu Hurairah (radhiAllahu 'anhu) said that Allaah'
s Messenger said, **"All of my Ummah will enter Paradise except those who refuse." It was said, "Who will refuse?" He replied. "Whoever obeys me enters Paradise and whoever**

disobeys me has refused.”

[Reported by al-Bukhaaree (Eng. trans. 9/284, no. 384)]

The Prophet (sallAllaahu 'alaihi wasallam) said, "Islaam began as something strange, and it shall return as something strange as it began. So Tooba (a tree in paradise) to the strangers." It was asked, "who are the strangers?" He replied, "those that purify and correct what the people have corrupted of my sunnah"

[Tabaraanee in al-Kabeer (6/202)]

The world cannot stop the way of Islam, all of the Muslims together following only the Prophet and respecting all of his companions.

The Prophet said, "Divine knowledge (light, the Sun) that rises in/from the east and sets in the west shall one day change its course"—we as Muslims truly believe that the sun will literally do this—"but first Allah (SWT) reveals through His signs and symbols; it shall rise in the west and continue until it reaches its climax, then after it reaches its

climax, it will return to its original course."
There has to be a paradigm shift before we
understand this saying of Prophet
Muhammad.

From: http://www.abovetopsecret.com

posted
on Aug,
27 2012
@ 07:35
AM link
In The Name of Allah, The Most Beneficent,
The Most Merciful
We seek refuge in Thee,
whomever Thou guides, none can
send astray, whomever Thou
sends astray none can guide.
Amen.

Islam is the only religion that
prophesies that the sun will rise
from the West, instead of from
rising from the East, in the the End
Times, before the Day of

Judgment. Both the Quran and the Hadith affirm that this phenomenon will take place. The occurrence of this phenomenon is considered in Islam as one of the major signs that indicate the Day of Judgment is close.

Allah says in the Qur'an:

"No good will it do to a person to believe then, if he believed not before, nor earn good (by performing deeds of righteousness) through his faith." (Surah Al-An'aam 6:158)

Abdullah-bin-Umar said, "I memorized a Hadith of the Messenger of Allah (pbuh) which I have not forgotten. I heard the Messenger of Allah (pbuh) say, 'The first of the Signs that will come is the rising of the sun from the place of its setting and the emergence of the Daabba to people in Duha (later portion of the morning before noon). Whichever of these two (signs) occurs before the other, then the other one will occur immediately after it."

Once the sun has risen from the West, the door of repentance for sins committed will be closed by

Allah and will remain closed until the Day of Judgement. The following Hadiths clearly specify that the deadline for repentance to be accepted by God ends when the sun rises from the West. Once the sun rises from the West, repentance will no longer be accepted.

Islam is rising in the west, and it is also the fastest growing religion (way of life) in the world. The proper way of understanding what the Prophet left us: his Sunnah, which is of him no more in the east except of those of the Salaafee: (the one sect that was prophesied to stay on the true ways taught by the prophet (SAW)). What he said is being understood more and more in the west. There is a pure way of understanding it here because of it being pure to the converts and *they* only wanting the part that is pure with no external influences. In the east, too many innovations that are added, as well as, to martyrdom: people adding prefixes to the word Muslim and terrorists believing that they are martyrs by blowing themselves up. The redirected direction of the divine knowledge of Islam will continue in the west until the east recognizes it and refocuses on the teaching of Prophet Muhammad; then the divine knowledge (light, the sun) will return on its original course. Before this happens, the east must first listen and relearn what Islam is: You must put aside your differences and go back to the Qu'ran and Sunnah together, then you must pay attention and do what Allah instructed us to do from the aspect of His words in the Qu'ran. The Qu'ran is the book of guidance to man, and Prophet Muhammad (SAW) is the example (best) of that guide.

Allah says, "Obey Me and My Prophet." Case in point! However you choose to understand that, so be it. None of the caliphs were prophets, and the only thing they could have or should have commanded is what Prophet Muhammad (SAW) commanded. This act makes them one with the Prophet. There was no division between Abu Bakr, Omar, Uthman, or Ali (ra). There should be no title in front of the word Muslim, because Muslim is the person and what that person should want to be, and Sunnah is the action of the Muslim. We should not be disputing who was to be followed after Allah (SWT) took Prophet Muhammad. The Prophet (SAW) was not a Sunni Muslim nor a Shiite Muslim or any other type of Muslim; he was simply a Muslim. We follow his way and his way alone; this is called his Sunnah, but it doesn't mean that we are Sunni Muslims. We are still simply Muslims that follow his Sunnah and his is the best example of this.

I am a Muslim; I submit to Islam by following the ways and teachings of Prophet Muhammad (SAW). Look at how division causes the east to kill each other by blowing themselves up along with innocent men, women, and children. See how they make friends with their enemies in peace and in war —and this because they allowed the west to come over there and divide them, now they are conquered by the west (divided and conquered). Muslim countries seek counsel from other nations and religions before they seek it from amongst the Quran and Sunnah themselves. The closest ally to a Sunni is another Muslim, even if he/she is Shiite. However, *they* have Americans, Europeans, Russians, and other friends to help *them* against *their* so-called Muslim enemies. Would *they* rather sleep with Shaytan?

The pillars of Islam are nothing but rituals to *them*. They are supposed to be the foundation of Islamic belief, so what is truly *their* foundation if the foundation *they* are supposed to have is only rituals?

Let me try this explanation: My Islamic foundation is my experience of meeting with

Prophet Muhammad (SAW). This is how I met him: I read books (*Muhammad,* by Hayykel, and *The Sealed Nectar*), the Bible numerous times, and the Noble Qu'ran likewise. With my studying, prayers, and faith, my knowing led me to practice and implement the Pillars of Islam into my worship. Allah did the rest by showing that as long as I did my part, He'd do

His. The Qu'ran became and is real to me, all of it manifest itself to those who believe truly.

Muhammad (SAW) did what he had to do and suffered what he had to suffer until the time came for him to take charge and fight oppression wherever it existed. He brought Muslims together and showed them how to handle all situations by Allah's permission. By Allah's permission, he is why we call ourselves Muslims. Allah has sent us into the world for a reason; from Him we all came, and to Him we all shall return. We are either Muslims or we are nothing. Who or what are we?

The Comforter
(Muhammad)

"The Comforter shall not come unto you"

John 16:7–15

Now I would like to share with you what only hope, grace and mercy can allow for you to perceive. It is the "sheep of a different fold." It is "the seed of the fertile ground that took root." It is "who lifts up the son of man." It is "the Comforter." It is Prophet Muhammad (SAW).

17 And the Lord said unto me, They have well spoken.

18 I will raise them up a Prophet from among their brethren like unto thee, and will put my words in his [j]mouth, and he shall speak unto them all that I shall command him.

19 And whosoever will not hearken unto my words, which he shall speak in my Name, I will [k]require it of him.

20 But the Prophet that shall presume to speak a word in my name, which I have not commanded him to speak, or that speaketh in the name of other gods, even the same Prophet shall die.

21 And if thou think in thine heart, How shall we know the word which the Lord hath not spoken?

22 When a Prophet speaketh in the Name of the Lord, if the thing [l]follow not nor come to pass, that is the thing which the Lord hath not spoken, but the Prophet hath spoken it presumptuously: thou shalt not therefore be afraid of him.17 And the Lord said unto me, They have well spoken.

18 I will raise them up a Prophet from among their brethren like unto thee, and will put my words in his [j]mouth, and he shall speak unto them all that I shall command him.

19 And whosoever will not hearken unto my words, which he shall speak in my Name, I will [k]require it of him.

20 But the Prophet that shall presume to speak a word in my name, which I have not commanded him to speak, or that speaketh in the name of other gods, even the same Prophet shall die.

21 And if thou think in thine heart, How shall we know the word which the Lord hath not spoken?

22 When a Prophet speaketh in the Name of the Lord, if the thing [l]follow not nor come to pass, that is the thing which the Lord hath not spoken, but the Prophet hath spoken presumptuously: thou shalt not therefore be afraid of him.

The Prophet Muhammad (SAW) is the

"prophet like Moses" more so than any other prophet. Moses married and had children. He had a mother and a father and led the children of Israel up out of Egypt through wars and conquered with Allah's help. He was given a book, the Torah. He died, and he is of the twelve tribes of Israel. The only prophet that is like this in every aspect is Prophet Muhammad (SAW): He married and had children. He had a mother and a father, and he led the Muslims up out of Mecca through wars and conquered with Allah's help. He was given a book: the Qu'ran. He died, and he is of the twelve princes of Ishmael, the brethren nation to the twelve tribes of Israel.

The Comforter is not the Holy Spirit. The Holy Spirit was not what Jesus was referring to when he spoke to his disciples. When you prophesy someone, you don't expose that person to his enemies by disclosing that person's name. It is a coded name that is broken after that person has come and, many times, after that person has left. This is why Jesus in the Old Testament is referred to as Christ, Emmanuel, the Messiah, and his name is nowhere mentioned. It is also why Prophet Muhammad (PBUH) is referred to as That Prophet, the spirit of truth, praiseworthy, the helper, and the Comforter. (See John 14:16–17 and other verses.)

The Prophet Muhammad (SAW) was no terrorist; he didn't kill innocent Muslims or any innocent others, for that matter. Though he was a warrior, he depended totally on Allah and Allah's strategy (plan), which was, is, and will be best. He was the truthful, the trustworthy, and he set the stage for us, by Allah's permission. He is our example for everything in this world by living the Qu'ran, and with his life, he showed us how we should live ours. By Allah, he gave us words of wisdom so that if we as one community would address life as a whole, we could defeat any enemy of Allah. He showed us that to submit, we have to obey, to obey we have to understand, to understand we have to learn, which in turn causes us to know, and by knowing, there is no hiding. Because Allah is our protection, He is our strength and our guide.

Prophet Muhammad's life is to be mimicked, copied, and projected— not just on an individual level, but especially today, as a family, neighborhood, community, city, nation, the whole world. There is a world out there today that is led by the enemy against righteousness. To fight it is to submit to Allah, but for the most part, we haven't done that because we haven't truly looked at the life of the Prophet (SAW). Though the odds were against him, he never went or even requested for anyone to go on a suicide mission. He always knew that Allah strengthened them with help from Himself. They never went into battle with the intentions to die, though they knew the chances were there; they were not afraid of becoming true martyrs. They did not throw themselves onto swords and did not in any way do things that even resemble taking their own lives the way that terrorists do these days, blowing themselves up just to get at others. He showed that the war was against the enemy and kept it free from those who had to stay at home and those who chose not to fight for whatever reason. It is no war if the war kills innocent people along with the enemy, even if you also have to die. That is nothing but terror.

If there are any mistakes or misrepresentation (not intended) of the truth in this manuscript, it is from myself as I've done my best to convey what is correct. If there is any truth which is intended in this manuscript it is solely from The Creator of all the worlds.

My Signature

It is in the flow of motion,

Given with much devotion,

Through all the threads of time,

And mine, I will cherish mine,

Twisted, turned, and even broken.,

The truth was even stolen,

And resurrected, reversed in the mind,

But your time is now to find.

Trust, faith, hope, and honesty,

Courage, obedience, and understanding;

Truth, truth, and truth.

Look in between the lines,

Add and deduce the rhymes,

And try to see your part.,

 Studying is a start.,

Poetry and writing are mine.,

This life has little time.,

Truth is in the art,

And you feel it in your heart.